THE JOURNEY TO EXCELLENCE IN LEGAL WRITING

Written by Pamela Newell and Timothy J. Peterkin

Edited by Brenda Gibson and Mary Wright

cognella™
San Diego, CA

First published in the United States of America in 2011 by Cognella, a division of University Readers, Inc.

Trademark Notice: Product or corporate names may be trademarks or registered trademarks, and are used only for identification and explanation without intent to infringe.

15 14 13 12 11   1 2 3 4 5

Printed in the United States of America.

ISBN: 978-1-609279-67-7

www.cognella.com 800.200.3908

DEDICATION

To my parents, McArthur and Dottie A. Newell, and my siblings, Regina Newell Stephens, Angela Newell Gray, Donna Y. Newell, McArthur Newell II, and Michael G. Newell.

—P.N.

To my mother, Mary S. Peterkin, and my father, Rocky E. Peterkin. Thank you for insisting that my life reflect a continuous journey to excellence, with no excuses. You are my constant motivation.

—T.J.P.

ACKNOWLEDGMENTS

Thank you to NCCU Legal Writing Director, Brenda Gibson, and Assistant Dean Wendy Scott, for their support. Thanks to Mary Wright, my mentor, for her invaluable help on this project. And my thanks to my coauthor, Timothy J. Peterkin, for his undying enthusiasm.

—P.N.

Thanks to my legal writing students for challenging and inspiring me. Thanks to my research assistants, Kevin Brockenbrough, Jordan Ford, Alvin Hudson, and Jamie Wilkerson. Thank you for being available to answer last-minute research questions and for providing countless hours of assistance. Thanks to the NCCU Legal Writing Program, the best in the country! Thank you to my coauthor, Pamela Newell, who always kept me focused and on track to meet deadlines.

—T.J.P.

FOREWORD

Law students across the country bemoan having to take Legal Research and Writing. I know this from my own first-hand experience as a student, a legal research and writing instructor, a professor of first-year students, and an academic dean. As Professors Newell and Peterkin suggest, new law students assume they can easily master legal writing. Those who are good writers assume that their research and writing skills are up to par, while not realizing the unique nature of legal research and writing. Other students have managed to mask fundamental writing problems, only to have them revealed in law school. The Journey to Excellence in Legal Writing addresses both the advanced and the challenged student writer.

Professors Newell and Peterkin deal thoroughly with fundamental grammar skills often overlooked in legal writing textbooks. The subsequent chapters cover everything that students should learn in legal writing, from spotting issues, finding and interpreting the law, to writing either an objective or persuasive document for their client or the court. Each chapter provides exhaustive treatment of the topic. The text also provides useful examples and exercises for the reader to test his or her understanding of the topic.

The Journey to Excellence in Legal Writing not only contains a thorough explication of legal writing for first-year law students. Upper-level students, practitioners, and judges will benefit from the instruction contained in these pages. I know that all readers will appreciate the organization, research, and writing in this book as much as I do. I plan to use the book myself, because a good writer never stops learning.

Wendy Scott
Associate Dean for Academic Affairs
NCCU School of Law

CONTENTS

Appendices

INTRODUCTION

Legal writing is the foundation of our profession, which rests on statutory and case law. Our statutes are carefully crafted by the legislature. Every word is there for a reason. When the courts determine that a statute is ambiguous, they proclaim it to be ambiguous and the legislature hastens to pass a clearer law. When our appellate courts, which provide case precedence, are the authors of incomprehensible opinions, they may be overruled by higher courts. Consequently, there is a need for excellence in legal writing. During and after law school, you should be able to show exemplary writing to the professor looking for scholarship, the judge reading your motion, the justice reading your brief, and the overworked senior partner reading your writing sample with appreciation.

Many students make the mistake of treating their first-year writing as a simple course, not worthy of the attention they give to doctrinal courses. Some hope that legal writing will be their "easy class." There are no easy classes in law school. Likewise, there are no unnecessary classes in law school. Every class is required or offered for a reason. There is a purpose for legal writing being a two- or three-semester course (or longer at some schools). You cannot fully understand law unless you can explain it. You learn to explain it in writing. If you have poor writing skills, you will have poor grades in every class that requires an essay exam or a term paper. Poor writing skills may follow your legal career by precluding you from unique jobs and opportunities. You are much less likely to obtain a clerkship for a judge or agency, you will make a poor associate, you cannot draft bills in the legislature, and a career in academia is highly unlikely. You will also fail to qualify for financial aid for scholarships requiring essays. Your legal correspondence will not effectively convey your skills as an attorney. Poor writing skills can also be costly in that you may be required to hire personnel to assist you in preparing your legal documents.

Thus, this text is dedicated to demonstrating perfect grammar, excellent citation and attribution characteristics, good legal writing habits, and interesting examples to illustrate the lessons. You will learn the differences between primary and secondary law, the doctrine of *stare decisis*, and the distinction between statutory law and case law. You will also become skilled at outlining rules in order to identify issues and craft issue statements properly. Additionally, you will gather knowledge to interpret statutes and apply case law to different factual scenarios. You will use synthesis to compare court holdings and reasoning in fashioning a general legal principle.

You will be taught how to develop organizational skills and use grammatical rules appropriately. In addition, you will be able to apply effective techniques in writing memoranda. You will study the importance of ethics in correspondence to a client. You will comprehend the power behind mediation and negotiations. You will study the best ways to answer examination questions.

The only way to improve your legal writing is by writing. Digest the chapters presented in this book and cultivate your writing skills. It is a valuable advantage in this profession. In fact, it is *a must*!

CHAPTER 1

✣

GRAMMAR

Many students are so eager to begin the process of legal writing that they bypass the rules of grammar. They believe that the legal analysis is the "meat and potatoes" of legal writing. While this is mostly true, the proper presentation of a document may be the difference between the meat and potatoes being served on a silver platter or a paper plate. Even for English and journalism majors, a grammar refresher is necessary. Think about how long it has been since you had a class on grammar. It has probably been a while, and you probably do not remember the rules precisely, as grammar is a precise subject. Do not make the mistake of believing the content of your writing will compensate for poor grammar. On the contrary, the poor grammar will, in all likelihood, lead the reader to disregard the substance of your writing. Do not allow your ideas to be dismissed so easily. After you have taken great strides to understand the legal analysis process, it would be unfortunate for the reader to lose confidence in your argument because of poor grammar. Using language accurately will make your writing easier to read and will focus the reader on your issue. You are responsible for knowing the rules of grammar. Thus, it is to your benefit to honestly assess the strength of your grammar and invest the necessary time to address any areas that need improvement.

For the time being, a short refresher is set below. Since most legal texts do not have a comprehensive grammar review, you should acquire a book that focuses solely on grammar.

1. MAKE SURE YOU DO NOT CONFUSE SIMILAR WORDS. FOR EXAMPLE:

a. Effect or affect

The word "effect" is a noun, meaning something that is produced by a cause. It is a result or consequence. For example: Exposure to the sun had the *effect* of toughening his skin. "Effect" also means the power to produce results or validity: His protest had no *effect*. "Effect" can be the state of being effective or operative: He anticipates bringing a plan into *effect*. "Effect" can also be defined as a mental or emotional impression produced, as by a painting or a speech.

On the contrary, "affect" is usually used as a verb. It means "to act on; produce an effect or change in something." Example: Cold weather *affected* the crops. "Affect" can also mean to impress the mind or move the feelings of: The music *affected* him deeply.

b. Lie or lay

Both words are verbs. However, the similarity ends there. To lie and to lay have very different meanings. "To lie" means to rest or assume or be situated in a horizontal position. "To lay" means to put or to place. Thus, the essential difference between these two verbs is that "to lie" describes an action undertaken by a subject, but it will never have a direct object, meaning the verb "to lie" does not express the kind of action that can be done to anything. See these sentence examples: (1) I like to *lie* in my hammock; (2) Yesterday, I *lay* there; and (3) I am *lying* on the sofa. "To lay" is never used to describe the act of reclining.

"To lay" is a transitive verb, needing a direct object because it describes an action that is done to something else. For example, something or someone has to be receiving the action of the verb "to lay." In other words, "to lay" is to place or to put. Examples: (1) I *lay* out my clothes for tomorrow the night before; (2) I will *lay* my books on the kitchen table tonight; and (3) I *laid* my blanket on the floor before I sat on it.

Frequently, students use "lay" when they should use lie, as in the sentence "I am going to lay down and rest." Instead, they should say "I am going to *lie* down and rest." Students also use "laid" when they should use "lay," as in the sentence "Fred laid in a hammock all afternoon watching the clouds." Instead, they should say "Fred *lay* in a hammock all afternoon." Tips to keep lie and lay straight: The verb that means "to recline" is to lie, not to lay. Thus, if we are talking about the act of reclining, we must use to lie, not to lay: "When I get a headache, I need to *lie* down and close my eyes." On the other hand, the verb "laid" will always have a direct object; for us to use the word "laid" correctly in a sentence, something or someone in the sentence must be getting "put" or "placed," as in the sentence: "I *laid* my car keys on the counter when I came home."

c. Sit or set

"To sit" is an intransitive verb, describing an action undertaken by the subject of a clause. However, it cannot take a direct object: the verb "to sit" does not express the kind of action that can be DONE TO anything. Just as with "to lie," think of "to sit" as meaning "to recline." Never use the words "sit" or "sat" to describe the act of putting or placing something or someone.

"To set" is a transitive verb, describing an action. It needs a direct object because it describes the kind of action that is DONE TO something. In other words, something or someone in the sentence has to be receiving the action expressed by the verb. Similar to the phrase "to lay," think of "to set" as meaning "to place or to put." Never use the word "set" to describe the act of reclining.

d. Which or that

Both words can be used in other constructions; however, they are easily confused when they are being used as pronouns to introduce clauses. Remember that a clause is simply a group of words containing a subject and a verb. Read the following sentences:

A. My car (*that* has a flat tire) needs servicing.
B. My car, (*which* has a flat tire), needs servicing.
C. The houses (*that* were renovated over the summer) are lovely.
D. The houses, (*which* were renovated over the summer), are lovely.

In all four sentences, the clause tells us something about either the car or the houses, but the choice of using "which" or "that" changes the way we should read each sentence. In Sentence A, the use of "that" suggests that the writer owns more than one car and therefore must explain to you which car she is referencing—the one with the flat tire. Consequently, the adjective clause is essential to your understanding of the sentence.

Sentence B tells the reader that she owns only one car and she is simply telling you that it happens to have a flat tire. That information is not necessary for the understanding of the sentence. In other words, without the adjective clause, the sentence would still make sense.

Sentence C provides that only SOME of the houses were renovated over the summer. If we omitted the clause "that were renovated over the summer," we would be left with "The houses are lovely." This statement would not be accurate because it implies that ALL the houses are lovely. Therefore, the adjective clause is essential to the meaning of the sentence. The writer is telling us that she is referencing ONLY the houses that were renovated over the summer—not the others.

In Sentence D, the clause is not essential because the sentence intends to tell us that ALL the houses were renovated. Further, the sentence would be clear even if the clause were omitted. To summarize, "which" clauses are nonessential. "That" clauses are essential. Nonessential clauses and phrases are set off from the rest of a sentence by a pair of commas.

e. Who or whom

"Who" and "whoever" are subjective pronouns. "Whom" and "whomever" are in the objective case. As simple and important as that distinction is, many people have difficulty regarding the proper usage of "who" and "whom." To keep them straight, remember that if you are able to substitute with "he" or "she," use "who." If "him" or "her" would be correct, use "whom."

Remember that every verb with a tense in a sentence must have a subject. That word is always in the nominative case, so you should use "who." Consider this sentence as an example: I decided to vote for *whoever* called me first. Here, "I" is the subject of "decided" and "he" is the subject of the verb "called." Consider another sentence: Give it to *whoever* deserves it: ([You] give it to whoever deserves it.) Here, "he" is the subject of the verb "deserves."

2. PUNCTUATION

a. Commas

Basic rules for comma usage: Use commas to separate independent clauses when they are joined by any of these seven coordinating conjunctions: and, but, for, or, nor, so, yet. Use commas after (a) introductory clauses; (b) phrases; or (c) words that come before the main clause. Use a pair of commas in the middle of a sentence to set off clauses, phrases, and words that are not essential to the meaning of the sentence. Use one comma before to indicate the beginning of the pause and one at the end to indicate the end of the pause.

Examples:
   a. David did not complete his homework, nor did he finish his chores.
   b. Even though the sky was cloudy, the meteorologist said that it would not rain.
   c. I looked fierce in my leather boots, which I got on sale, and my matching leather coat.
   d. Before the holidays, I need to shop for gifts, groceries, cards, and stockings.
   e. Donna was a happy, healthy baby.
   f. For my birthday, I rented a club, contacted a caterer, and signed an agreement with a deejay.

Use commas to separate three or more words, phrases, or clauses written in a series. Use commas to separate two or more coordinate adjectives that describe the same noun. Be sure never to add an extra comma between the final adjective and the noun itself or to use commas with non-coordinate adjectives. Use a comma near the end of a sentence to separate contrasted coordinate elements or to indicate a distinct pause or shift. Use commas to set off phrases at the end of the sentence that refer to the beginning or middle of the sentence. Such phrases are free modifiers that can be placed anywhere in the sentence without causing confusion. Use commas to set off all geographical names, items in dates (except the month and day), addresses (except the street number and name), and titles in names. Use commas to separate three or more words, phrases, or clauses written in a series.

Do not use commas to set off essential elements of the sentence, such as clauses beginning with "that." "That" clauses after nouns are always essential. "That" clauses following a verb expressing mental action are always essential. Do not use a comma to separate the subject from the verb. Do not put a comma between the two verbs or verb phrases in a compound predicate. Do not put a comma between the two nouns, noun phrases, or noun clauses in a compound subject or compound object. Do not put a comma after the main clause when a dependent (subordinate) clause follows it (except for cases of extreme contrast).

b. Semicolons

Students often attempt to write complex sentences. While shorter, simpler sentences are preferred, complex sentences are acceptable as long as they are punctuated correctly and the meaning is clear to the reader.

If you have two independent clauses in one sentence, you must separate them with a semicolon.

Example: Michelle threw the ball at Jon; however, the ball struck Jon's dog first.

Example: The issue is whether Michelle will be found liable for Jon's dog's injuries when Michelle threw the ball; the ball hit the dog; and the dog cannot recover on its own.

3. SUBJECT-VERB AGREEMENT

When the subject of a sentence is composed of two or more nouns or pronouns connected by "and," use a plural verb. When two or more singular nouns or pronouns are connected by "or" or "nor," use a singular verb. When a compound subject contains both a singular and a plural noun or pronoun joined by "or" or "nor," the verb should agree with the part of the subject that is nearer the verb.

"Doesn't" is a contraction of "does not" and should be used only with a singular subject. "Don't" is a contraction of "do not" and should be used only with a plural subject. The exception to this rule appears in the case of the first person and second person pronouns

"I" and "you." With these pronouns, the contraction "don't" should be used. Please note that contractions are rarely proper in legal writing.

Do not be misled by a phrase that comes between the subject and the verb. The verb agrees with the subject, not with a noun or pronoun in the phrase. For example: "One of the boxes is open." The words "each," "each one," "either," "neither," "everyone," "everybody," "anybody," "anyone," "nobody," "somebody," "someone," and "no one" are singular and require a singular verb. For example: "Either is correct."

Nouns such as civics, mathematics, dollars, measles, and news require singular verbs. Nonetheless, when discussing money you need to use a singular verb, but when referring to the dollars themselves, a plural verb is required. Nouns such as scissors, tweezers, trousers, and shears require plural verbs because there are two parts to these items. In sentences beginning with "there is" or "there are," the subject follows the verb. Since "there" is not the subject, the verb agrees with what follows. For example: (1) There are many questions; and (2) There is a question.

Collective nouns are words that imply more than one person but are considered singular and take a singular verb, such as: group, team, committee, class, and family. Expressions such as "with," "together with," "including," "accompanied by," "in addition to," or "as well" do not change the number of the subject. Remember, if the subject is singular, the verb is also.

4. PLURALS, POSSESSIVES, AND POSSESSIVE PLURALS

Usually a writer can show possession by using an apostrophe. However, students become confused when making plural nouns or nouns ending in "s" possessive. When showing the possessive of a pluralized family name, you must pluralize it first and then simply make the name possessive with the use of an apostrophe. For example, "You might ride in the Smiths' car when we visit the Joneses at the Joneses' home."

For expressions of time and measurement, the possessive is shown with an apostrophe "s." For example, see: "one dollar's worth," "two dollars' worth," "a hard day's night," "two years' experience," "an evening's entertainment," and "two weeks' notice." With nouns whose plurals are irregular, add an apostrophe followed by an "s" to create the possessive form. For example: (1) She plans on opening a women's clothing boutique; (2) Children's programming is not a high priority; and (3) The geese's food supply was endangered.

5. TRANSITIONS

Good transitions can connect paragraphs and turn disconnected writing into a unified whole, by helping readers understand how paragraphs work together, reference one another, and build to a larger point. The key to producing good transitions is highlighting connections between corresponding paragraphs. By referencing in one paragraph the relevant material from previous ones; writers can develop important points for their readers.

It is a good idea to continue one paragraph where another ends. Picking up key phrases from the previous paragraph and highlighting them in the next can create an obvious progression for readers. Many times, it only takes a few words to draw these connections. Instead of writing transitions that could connect any paragraph to any other paragraph, write a transition that could only connect one specific paragraph to another specific paragraph.

a. **Add**: and, again, and then, besides, equally important, finally, further, furthermore, nor, too, next, lastly, what's more, moreover, in addition, first (second, etc.)
b. **Compare**: whereas, but, yet, on the other hand, however, nevertheless, on the contrary, by comparison, where, compared to, up against, balanced against, vis à vis, but, although, conversely, meanwhile, after all, in contrast, although this may be true
c. **Prove**: because, for, since, for the same reason, evidently, furthermore, moreover, besides, indeed, in fact, in addition, in any case, that is
d. **Show Exception**: yet, still, however, nevertheless, in spite of, despite, of course, once in a while, sometimes, occasionally
e. **Show Time**: immediately, thereafter, soon, after a few hours, finally, then, later, previously, formerly, first (second, etc.), next, and then
f. **Repeat**: in brief, as has been noted
g. **Emphasize**: definitely, extremely, in fact, indeed, in any case, absolutely, positively, naturally, surprisingly, always, forever, perennially, eternally, never, emphatically, unquestionably, without a doubt, certainly, undeniably, without reservation
h. **Show Sequence**: first, second, third, and so forth. A, B, C, and so forth, next, then, following this, at this time, now, at this point, after, afterward, subsequently, finally, consequently, previously, before this, simultaneously, concurrently, thus, therefore, hence, next, and then, soon
I. **Give an Example**: for example, for instance, in this case, in another case, on this occasion, in this situation, take the case of, to demonstrate, to illustrate, as an illustration, to illustrate
J. **Summarize or Conclude**: in brief, on the whole, summing up, to conclude, in conclusion, hence, therefore, accordingly, thus, as a result, consequently, on the whole

6. NOUN-PRONOUN AGREEMENT

When using a singular pronoun, you must also use a singular noun. While this sounds simple, often students err because they are actually seeking to remain gender-neutral.

Incorrect: When *a parent* is acting inconsistently with *their* constitutionally protected status as a parent, third parties may gain custody rights.

Correct: When *parents are* acting inconsistently with *their* constitutionally protected status as a parent, third parties may gain custody rights.

Correct: When *a parent* is acting inconsistently with *his or her* constitutionally protected status as a parent, third parties may gain custody rights.

Frequently, students realize it is politically incorrect to refer to a gender-neutral noun with a specific pronoun. Although this is true, it remains inappropriate to refer to the singular pronoun with a plural noun.

Additional grammar tips are located in the Appendix.

CHAPTER 2

✝

SOURCES OF LAW: PRIMARY AND SECONDARY AUTHORITY

PRIMARY AUTHORITY

Primary sources of law come from statutes and case law. Statutes are legislative laws that the legislators codify in statute books. Case law is formed when an appellate court either interprets a statute to explain its meaning, or applies a statute to a set of facts in an opinion. Statutes do not only provide punishment for criminal offenses. They can create public offices, remedies to actions and exceptions to a rule. Statutes can also be a response from the people about how an appellate court ruled in a certain case. Statutes can provide monetary assistance to state entities. For example, look at this statute that provides for a guardian *ad litem* to represent a child in court:

N.C. Gen. Stat. § 7B-600. Appointment of guardian.

(a) In any case when no parent appears in a hearing with the juvenile or when the court finds it would be in the best interests of the juvenile, the court may appoint a guardian of the person for the juvenile. The guardian shall operate under the supervision of the court with or without bond and shall file only such reports as the court shall require. The guardian shall have the care, custody, and control of the juvenile or may arrange a suitable placement for the juvenile and may represent the juvenile in legal actions before any court. The guardian may consent to certain actions on the part of the juvenile in place of the parent including (i) marriage, (ii) enlisting in the Armed Forces, and (iii) enrollment in school. The guardian may also consent to any necessary remedial, psychological, medical, or surgical treatment for the juvenile. The authority of the guardian shall continue until the guardianship is terminated by court order, until the juvenile is emancipated pursuant to Article 35 of Subchapter IV of this Chapter, or until the juvenile reaches the age of majority.

Here is a statute prohibiting and defining burglary:

N.C. Gen. Stat. § 14-51 Burglary.

There shall be two degrees in the crime of burglary as defined at the common law. If the crime be committed in a dwelling house, or in a room used as a sleeping apartment in any building, and any person is in the actual occupation of any part of said dwelling house or sleeping apartment at the time of the commission of such crime, it shall be burglary in the first degree. If such crime be committed in a dwelling house or sleeping apartment not actually occupied by anyone at the time of the commission of the crime, or if it be committed in any house within the curtilage of a dwelling house or in any building not a dwelling house, but in which is a room used as a sleeping apartment and not actually occupied as such at the time of the commission of the crime, it shall be burglary in the second degree. For the purposes of defining the crime of burglary, larceny shall be deemed a felony without regard to the value of the property in question.

Frequently, the state legislature will pass a bill in response to current events. For example, after Jessica Lunsford, a minor, was raped by an adult, the N.C. General Assembly passed the Jessica Lunsford Act. The Act, found in section 14-27.2A of the general statutes, increases the penalties for certain sexual offenses committed against children, including longer sentences and lifetime electronic monitoring. It also makes sex offender registration requirements more stringent and makes it unlawful for a sex offender to be on certain premises.

The legislature may enact a law regarding a statewide or national problem. For example, in August 2009, the House and Senate both approved HB 945, known as the Study Bill. It contains authorization to create the "Legislative Task Force on Childhood Obesity." The bill was directed to address the problem of childhood obesity and encourage healthy eating and increased physical activity among children. The law provided funding for early childhood intervention, comprehensive nutrition education in schools, and increased access to recreational activities for children.

The legislature may also pass laws based on a court's interpretation of a statute. In 1999, the Maryland Court of Appeals considered *Burch v. United Cable Television*, 354 Md. 658, 732 A.2d 887 (1999), a case where a cable customer sued because the local cable company charged a five-dollar late fee. At the time of the action, the law was that "such late fees could not be charged in excess of six percent per annum without authorization from the General Assembly." In response, the Maryland legislature enacted section 14-1315 of the Commercial Law Article, allowing an increase in late fees in 2006.

SECONDARY AUTHORITY

Secondary sources of law come from other jurisdictions and handbooks. These should only be used in addition to primary sources unless you are discussing an issue of first impression. Sometimes, secondary sources can be used to bolster your argument and add a little more persuasiveness to an argument. For example:

> In North Carolina, damages for claims of alienation of affections and criminal conversation are limited to the present value in money of the support, consortium, and other legally protected marital interests lost due to a defendant's actions. *Hutelmyer v. Cox*, 133 N.C. App. 364, 514 S.E.2d 554 (2000). South Dakota allows punitive damages. *Veeder v. Kennedy*, 589 N.W.2d 610 (S.D.,1999). In *Veeder*, the trial court allowed a $200,000 punitive damage award. However, some jurisdictions, such as New York, do not allow money as damages for alienation of affections. *Marmelstein v. Kehillat New Hempstead*, 45 A.D.3d 33, 841 N.Y.S.2d 493 (2007). Therefore, this Court should consider limiting damages to only money.

The secondary sources here are used as persuasive authority, not direct authority or precedence.

Precedence

Primary sources may be used as precedent in your arguments. If a court has ruled on a certain issue in a certain way (e.g., under the automobile exception of the Fourth Amendment, law enforcement does not need a search warrant to search your car), then you do not need to reinvent the wheel. You may cite to a case with precedent in favor of your argument. "Precedent" is defined as an authoritative decision, authoritative principle of law, or an established legal doctrine. Sources are never precedent if they come from a different jurisdiction. However, they may be used as persuasive authority as in the example above. Secondary sources include case law from other jurisdictions, statutes from other jurisdictions, law review articles, legal journals, and other types of legal scholarship.

Precedent will ordinarily govern the decision of a later similar case, unless a party can show that it was wrongly decided or that it differed in some significant way. Precedent that must be applied or followed is known as "binding." Under the doctrine of *stare decisis*, a lower court must follow findings of law made by a higher court in that jurisdiction. A lower court is prohibited from making its own interpretation where a higher court has already interpreted the issue. However, decisions of lower courts are not binding on each other or any courts higher in the system. Moreover, appeals court decisions are not binding on other appeals courts or on lower courts in other jurisdictions. It should be noted that occasionally, a higher court will adopt the reasoning and conclusion of a lower court. Give an example using the Wake County District versus Durham County District. Use Eastern District v. Middle District.

Additionally, courts must follow their own previous interpretations of law. In other words, one panel of an intermediate appellate court in South Dakota cannot deviate from a previous decision on an issue in the intermediate appellate court in South Dakota.

Stare decisis is only mandatory where a case is "directly on point," or specifically considers the identical issue in a case with almost identical or similar facts. In extraordinary circumstances, a higher court may overturn or overrule mandatory precedent, but will usually limit the rule to a narrow interpretation. The higher court will also attempt to distinguish the precedent before reversing it.

Discussion questions:

1. Why would it be problematic if courts within the same jurisdiction had different precedent they used in considering cases?

2. Why are trial court orders and judgments not binding on other trial courts in the same jurisdiction?

3. Why would you not want to base your entire argument on secondary sources?

CHAPTER 3

✝

OUTLINING RULES AND ISSUE IDENTIFICATION

CONJUNCTIVE TEST

There are several types of rules: conjunctive, disjunctive, totality of the circumstances, balancing and weighing factors and the plain meaning rule. In a conjunctive test, elements of a law are considered. Every element must be present in order for that specific law to apply. For example, in the following statute, the prosecution may only convict someone of appropriation if all of the elements in the statute prohibiting appropriation are present:

> Any person engaged in a partnership business in the State of North Carolina who, without the knowledge and consent of his copartner or copartners, take funds belonging to the partnership business and appropriates the same to his own personal use with the fraudulent intent of depriving his copartners of the use thereof, shall be guilty of a felony.

In order for this rule to be applicable, the prosecution must show that a defendant engaged in the prohibited conduct. Ask yourself: In general, to whom does this statute apply?

Any person engaged in a partnership business in the State of North Carolina who, without the knowledge and consent of his copartner or copartners, take funds belonging to the partnership business and appropriates the same to his own personal use with the fraudulent intent of depriving his copartners of the use thereof, shall be guilty of a felony.

Specifically, to whom does this statute apply?

Any person engaged in a partnership business *in the State of North Carolina* who, without the knowledge and consent of his copartner or copartners, take funds belonging to the partnership business and appropriates the same to his own personal use with the fraudulent intent of depriving his copartners of the use thereof, shall be guilty of a felony.

How does this statute affect the applicable people? It prohibits certain actions. The applicable people cannot:

1. Without the knowledge
2. And consent of the other partners
3. Take funds
4. Belonging to the partnership and appropriate the funds to his own personal use
5. With the fraudulent intent of depriving his copartners of the use of the money

If all of the elements are shown, then the person will be guilty of a felony. A conjunctive rule test will have the rule outline thusly.

DISJUNCTIVE TEST

A disjunctive test is an either/or test. For example: A lawyer shall not collect a contingent fee in a criminal matter OR a divorce. The outline of the rule should look like this:

Rule: A lawyer shall not collect a contingent fee in a criminal matter or a divorce.

Outline: A lawyer shall not collect a contingent fee in either of the following kinds of cases:

A. a criminal matter OR
B. a divorce

TOTALITY OF THE CIRCUMSTANCES TEST

The totality of the circumstances test considers multiple factors. For example:

Rule: Child custody shall be decided in accordance with the best interest of the child. Factors to consider in deciding the best interests of the child are: the fitness of each possible custodian; the appropriateness for parenting of the lifestyle of each possible custodian; the relationship between the child and each possible custodian; the placement of the child's siblings, if any; living accommodations; the district lines of the child's school; the proximity of extended family and friends; religious issues; any other factors relevant to the child's best interests.

All of these factors should be considered in developing a conclusion.

BALANCING TEST

A balancing test considers juxtaposed factors. For example:

Rule: A party must respond to properly propounded interrogatories unless the burden of responding substantially outweighs the questioning party's legitimate need for the information. To measure "burden," the judge might consider a number of factors, such as the time and effort necessary to answer; the cost of compiling the information; any privacy concerns of the objecting party; and any other circumstances particular to the objecting party's situation. To measure "legitimate need," the judge might consider a number of other factors, such as how important the information would be to the issues of trial, whether the information would be available from some other source or in some other form, and any other circumstances relating to the party's need for the information.

Outline: A party must respond to properly propounded interrogatories unless the burden of responding substantially outweighs the questioning party's legitimate need for the information.

The burden of answering:

1. Time and effort necessary to answer
2. Cost of compiling the information
3. Any privacy concerns of the objecting party
4. Any other circumstances raised by that particular party's situation

VERSUS

The questioning party's need for information:

5. How important the information would be to the issues of the trial
6. Whether the information would be available from some other source or in some other form
7. Any other circumstances relating to the party's need for the information

PLAIN MEANING RULE

This test is set out like a command. These are rules that have no elements, factors, or other subparts. For example: To be valid, a will must be signed. Another example follows:

Rule: A lawyer shall not prepare any document giving the lawyer a gift from a client except where the gift is insubstantial or where the client is related to the lawyer.

Outline: A lawyer shall not prepare any document giving the lawyer a gift from a client except:

1. Where the gift is insubstantial, OR
2. Where the client is related to the lawyer

Note: This is an example of a rule with one or more exceptions.

As you can see, in order to best understand a statute or rule from a case, you should outline the rule by breaking it down word by word and/or phrase by phrase. Complete the practice examples in Appendix I.

In properly analyzing a legal problem, you must first know what rule to apply and what is at issue in the rule. Frequently, this type of assignment helps you narrow the facts and questions of law down to just what needs to be analyzed. Then you are able to discard extraneous material that is not at issue.

Example Rule: A person is liable for battery when she intentionally causes a harmful or offensive contact with the person of another or anything so closely connected with the other's body as to be regarded a part of it.

Fact Pattern: Louis Thomas, a die-hard Dallas Cowboys fan, was walking down the sidewalk. He saw Jennifer Riley walking toward him. Jennifer was wearing a Washington Redskins' cap. The Redskins are dedicated rivals of the Cowboys. As Louis passed Jennifer, he intentionally struck the brim of her cap, knocking it off of her head. The blow caused Jennifer to lose her balance and she fell and broke her arm. Can she successfully bring a civil claim of battery against Louis?

> Step 1. What is the rule in the fact pattern?
> Step 2. Break down the rule into single elements. "A person is liable for battery when she intentionally causes a harmful or offensive contact with the person of another or anything so closely connected with the other's body as to be regarded a part of it."

Outline: A person is liable for battery when she

1. intentionally causes a
2. harmful or offensive
3. contact
4. with the person of another or
5. anything so closely connected with the other's body as to be regarded a part of it

> Step 3. Determine which elements of the rule are at issue. Look at the facts and see if there is any dispute as to that issue.

a. Did Louis act intentionally? Yes. This fact is not disputed, so the first element is not at issue.
b. Was Louis's action harmful or offensive? Yes, because it caused Jennifer to fall and break her arm.
c. Did Louis have contact with Jennifer? Yes, so this element as well is not at issue.
d. Was Louis's contact with Jennifer's person? No. He only came in contact with Jennifer's cap. Therefore, this is not at issue.
e. Was Jennifer's cap so closely connected with her body as to be a part of her body? Maybe. You can argue this one either way. When you can make an argument (whether you agree with it or not), then that element is at issue. Accordingly, your outline should look like this:

Rule: A person is liable for battery when she
1. intentionally causes a **(no issue)**
     Facts: Louis intentionally struck Jennifer's cap.
2. harmful or offensive **(no issue)**
     Facts: Jennifer fell and broke her arm.
3. contact **(no issue)**
     Facts: Louis struck Jennifer's cap.

4. with the person of another or **(no issue)**
    Facts: Louis did not make contact with Jennifer's person.
5. anything so closely connected with the other's body as to be regarded a part of it **(issue)**
    Facts: Jennifer was walking with a cap on her head.

    Step 4. Consequently, your analysis will discuss only the fifth element. You must formulate your issue statement around this element. Do not include the other four elements because they are not questioned here.

Look at the following example and complete the exercises. Here, your law will come from a case, *Polo Fashions, Inc. v. Craftex, Inc.* Read the case and outline the rule of law therein.

Facts:

Geoff Thomas, owner of Stringz, Inc., has come to you seeking advice regarding laws on deceptive advertising. He presents you with the following facts:

Goodfellas, a popular department store, sells purses. In 2006, Goodfellas stocked many brands of purses, including Stringz, a popular, upscale brand. Stringz purses are all black leather, but in different shapes and sizes. Stringz's logo is a crochet needle with a loose string of yarn. In 2007, Goodfellas signed an exclusive contract with Threadz, which also manufactures purses. The Threadz purses come only in black vinyl and are in various shapes and sizes. The Threadz logo is an unraveling spool of thread.

The average Stringz purse retails at approximately $500.00. The average Threadz purse retails at approximately $60.00 Goodfellas believes that it is getting a great bargain by using Threadz purses instead of Stringz purses. However, some customers have complained that Goodfellas sold them Threadz purses when they believed that they were buying Stringz purses.

Therefore, Goodfellas placed Stringz purses randomly amongst the Threadz purses. In a typical store, there were approximately 1,000 purses on the racks. Of the 1,000 purses, approximately 100 were Stringz purses. The others were made by Threadz. Stringz noticed that it is not making the same amount of money from Goodfellas as it makes with other department stores with a similar contract. Customers who would normally buy Stringz purses are buying Threadz purses because they are more inexpensive.

In 2006, Stringz made $300,000.00 from purses sold in Goodfellas Department Store. In 2007, it made $78,000.00. Threadz made $200,000.00 in 2007.

You have one case on point, *Polo Fashions, Inc. v. Craftex, Inc.*,* which is relevant to your facts as presented by Mr. Thomas. Read the case and pull out the relevant rule.

POLO FASHIONS, INC. v. CRAFTEX, INC.
April 9, 1987.

HAYNSWORTH, Senior Circuit Judge:

This is an action for trademark infringement under the Lanham Act and for unfair competition in pendent state law claims. The district court awarded summary judgment to the plaintiff on the question of liability. On the defendant's appeal we affirm the judgment.

I. Polo Fashions is a well-known fashion house selling clothing for men and women designed by Ralph Lauren. On its labels, the company uses its trademarks and trade names POLO, RALPH LAUREN and POLO BY RALPH LAUREN. It also uses extensively a fanciful embroidered representation of a polo player mounted on a horse. On knitted sport shirts, such as those with which we are concerned, the polo player symbol typically appears on the breast of the shirt.

The plaintiff's merchandise enjoys a reputation for quality. It appears to have been imitated with some frequency, and the plaintiff has successfully defended its trademarks and symbols against alleged infringers.

Defendant, Craftex, Inc., is a manufacturer of knit shirts. In 1982 and 1983, Craftex manufactured and sold 1,388 dozen knit sport shirts bearing an embroidered emblem substantially identical to the plaintiff's polo player symbol.

The plaintiff filed this action alleging unfair trade practices under North Carolina's Unfair Trade Practices Act, N.C. Gen. Stat. § 75-1.1 (1985) which provides that:

a. Unfair methods of competition in or affecting commerce, and unfair or deceptive acts or practices in or affecting commerce, are declared unlawful.

b. For purposes of this section, "commerce" includes all business activities, however denominated, but does not include professional services rendered by a member of a learned profession.

c. Nothing in this section shall apply to acts done by the publisher, owner, agent, or employee of a newspaper, periodical or radio or television station, or other advertising medium in the publication or dissemination of an advertisement, when the owner, agent or employee did not have knowledge of the false, misleading or deceptive character of the advertisement and when the newspaper, periodical or radio or television station, or other advertising medium did not have a direct financial interest in the sale or distribution of the advertised product or service.

---

* Case altered for educational purposes.

d. Any party claiming to be exempt from the provisions of this section shall have the burden of proof with respect to such claim.

After a bench trial, the district court found that the defendants made a profit of $14,837.72 in the manufacture and sale of the accused shirts. It found the plaintiff had suffered damages in that amount, and it then trebled the damages under North Carolina's Unfair Trade Practices Act in N.C. Gen. Stat. 75-16:

> If any person shall be injured or the business of any person, firm or corporation shall be broken up, destroyed or injured by reason of any act or thing done by any other person, firm or corporation in violation of the provisions of this Chapter, such person, firm or corporation so injured shall have a right of action on account of such injury done, and if damages are assessed in such case judgment shall be rendered in favor of the plaintiff and against the defendant for treble the amount fixed by the verdict.

II. The plaintiff's symbol, standing alone, is a strong mark of the identity of the source. *See, e.g., Gordon Group*, 627 F.Supp. at 887. It has been widely used by the plaintiff and, as indicated above, has not infrequently been imitated. The strength of the mark is the "first and paramount factor" in assessing the likelihood of confusion. *Pizzeria Uno*, 747 F.2d at 1527. In this case, the two symbols are substantially identical. They are used in the same manner on the breast of the same product, knitted sport shirts. Where, as here, one produces counterfeit goods in an apparent attempt to capitalize upon the popularity of, and demand for, another's product, there is a presumption of a likelihood of confusion. *See AMP, Inc. v. Foy*, 540 F.2d 1181, 1186 (4th Cir.1976).

The North Carolina unfair trade practices statute prohibits unfair methods of competition and unfair or deceptive acts or practices. N.C. Gen. Stat. § 75-1.1 (1985). As used in the statute, the words "unfair methods of competition," have not been precisely defined by the North Carolina courts, although it has been suggested that they encompass any conduct that a court of equity would consider unfair.

Defendants contend, however, that there was no likelihood of confusion because of a label affixed inside the back of the neck of each shirt bearing the words Knight of Armor. The plaintiff never used such a mark as Knight of Armor, but even the most sophisticated purchaser, seeing the polo player symbol on the front of the shirt, might suppose the plaintiff had adopted another trademark in addition to POLO, RALPH LAUREN, and POLO BY RALPH LAUREN. Moreover, in the after sale context, one seeing the shirt being worn by its owner, would not see the label on the back of the neck. Seeing the polo player symbol, it is likely that the observer would identify the shirt with the plaintiff, and the plaintiff's reputation would suffer damage if the shirt appeared to be of poor quality. *See Lois Sportswear U.S.A., Inc. v. Levi Strauss & Co.*, 799 F.2d 867 (2d Cir.1986).

On the facts of this case, we think that the likelihood of confusion was so unassailably established as to warrant the district court's entry of summary judgment for the plaintiff as to liability. Plaintiff was entitled to such an award upon its common law claim of unfair competition and its claim under North Carolina's Unfair Trade Practices Act. In addition, the trial court did not err in trebling Plaintiff's damages.

It cannot be said that the defendants' infringement caused the plaintiff to lose the sales of the number of shirts sold by the defendants. Nor can it be said that the plaintiff lost sales equivalent to the total dollar sales of the shirts by the defendants. The retail price of plaintiff's shirts was several times the retail price at which the defendants' goods were sold. It is more than likely that some buyers of the defendants' shirts would not have been willing to pay the higher price necessary to purchase one of the plaintiff's shirts. That the plaintiff's sales were adversely affected, however, can hardly be denied. Nor is the injury suffered by the plaintiff in its reputation for its goods mathematically convertible into a fixed dollar amount, but it is hardly to be denied that some such injury occurred. Under these circumstances, instead of having a fact finder assess damages with little guidance, fairness to the infringers suggests strongly that the plaintiff's damages should be limited to the defendants' profits, and that is what was done. The district court properly treated the award as damages suffered by the plaintiff, and trebled that amount under the North Carolina statute.

AFFIRMED IN PART AND REVERSED IN PART.

1. What is the rule in the Polo case?
2. Looking at the facts, determine what part of the rule is at issue.
3. Formulate an issue statement.

1. Compare your answers and outline with those below.

The rule is taken from N.C. Gen. Stat. § 75-1.1:

a. Unfair methods of competition in or affecting commerce, and unfair or deceptive acts or practices in or affecting commerce, are declared unlawful.

b. For purposes of this section, "commerce" includes all business activities, however denominated, but does not include professional services rendered by a member of a learned profession.

c. Nothing in this section shall apply to acts done by the publisher, owner, agent, or employee of a newspaper, periodical or radio or television station, or other advertising medium in the publication or dissemination of an advertisement, when the owner, agent or employee did not have knowledge of the false, misleading or deceptive character of the advertisement and when the newspaper, periodical or radio or television station, or other advertising medium did not have a direct financial interest in the sale or distribution of the advertised product or service.

d. Any party claiming to be exempt from the provisions of this section shall have the burden of proof with respect to such claim.

2. Outline:

a. Unfair or deceptive acts
b. in business are declared unlawful
c. In determining whether the statute has been violated, the trial court must consider the
   i. appearance of trademark
   ii. the popularity of trademark, and
   iii. the location of trademark

3. Add relevant facts:

a. **Unfair or deceptive acts**
   The Threadz and Stringz purses contained similar features.
   The Stringz purse cost $500.00 and the Threadz purse cost $200.00.
   Customers complained Goodfellas sold them Threadz when they thought they were buying Stringz.
   Goodfellas deliberately mixed the purses together.

b. **In business are declared unlawful**
   Goodfellas is a department store.
   Stringz manufactures purses.
   Threadz manufactures purses.

c. **In determining whether the statute has been violated, the trial court must consider the:**
   i. **appearance of trademark;**
   The Threadz trademark is an unraveling spool of thread. The Stringz trademark is similar to a crochet needle with a loose string of yarn.
   ii. **the popularity of trademark;**
   Stringz well-known to professional women. Stringz established in 1950
   Threadz well-known to teens and young adults

Threadz established in 1982
iii.   the location of trademark.
Not apparent from outside the purse.
Located on inside of purse.

4.   Which elements are at issue?

a.   **Unfair or deceptive acts**

Not an issue because the facts here are not disputed.

b.   **in business are declared unlawful**

Not an issue. It is clear that the parties are engaged in business.

c.   **In determining whether the statute has been violated, the trial court must consider:**

i. the appearance of trademark;

An issue because it can be argued that the spool looked substantially different from a crochet needle and loose yarn.

ii. the popularity of trademark;

An issue because one brand is popular with one generation and the other is popular with a younger generation, but that may not mean that the trademarks are universally popular.

iii. the location of trademark.

Not an issue because the trademark is inside the purse and not apparent from the outside. Thus, shoppers would not have considered the trademark when purchasing, because it is not visible.

CHAPTER 4

✝

ISSUE FORMULATION

Once you have correctly identified the issue, the next step is to properly formulate the issue statement. There is good news here. First, the issue statement is only one sentence. You only address one issue per issue statement. There are only two possible formats for the issue statement. The issue statement only has three components: the legal question, governing law, and the relevant facts. Take these components and present them in the form of a statement or question answerable by a "yes" or "no," and the issue statement has been formulated.

The main purpose of the issue statement is to give the reader a preview of the analysis. The document will be presented to other attorneys or judges. They also have a basic understanding of the law and legal analysis. The proper issue statement gives the reader a proper framework in which to read the memorandum. After reading the issue statement, the reader should have confidence that you have a command of the issue to be analyzed. The reader will know that you have identified the appropriate laws to be addressed, you have narrowed down the macro issue and will address the micro issue for the reader, and you know the facts that are relevant to the discussion.

The first component of the issue statement is the law. The law that you are referencing can be any law that is relevant to the issue you have identified. Be sure to note that any relevant source of law can be placed in this section. See the previous chapter on sources of law. In your reference to the source of law, be as specific as possible, without excluding relevant portions of the law. At the time you create your issue statement, you should have a working knowledge of the law that will be analyzed to answer the legal question being presented. For example, it would be unacceptable to state "under North Carolina law..." or "under the United States constitution..." At the same time, if you have identified a particularly relevant section of statutes, you do not need to list all of the statutes that may be relevant. If you are going to reference a foreclosure matter, it is sufficient to reference the section of the foreclosure statutes, i.e., "under Chapter 45 of the N.C. General Statutes..." It would be inappropriate to reference a specific statute or case if your analysis will address more than that law. For example, do not state "under N.C. Gen. Stat. § 45-21.15..." if your analysis addresses other statutes. Stating only part of the law that will be addressed does not give the readers the full preview of what will be addressed in the analysis.

The next component of the issue statement is the legal question. This is the "issue" you have already identified based on the process you learned in the previous chapter. This is the "micro issue." It is fairly specific. The appropriate legal question is never whether someone is liable or guilty. In every civil case, there is a question of liability. Asking about basic liability in the issue statement gives the readers no meaningful preview of the analysis. Similarly, in every criminal case, there is a question of guilt. For example, do not state: "Under N.C. Gen. Stat. 45-21 et seq. is the lender liable..." If the case is about a lender violating state lending laws, the ultimate question will always be about liability. Give the reader a more in-depth look at what you are addressing in the analysis. If the issue is regarding a lender's possible violation of state lending laws, the issue is not simply whether the lender is liable for a violation of the law. More particularly, are you addressing whether the lender has charged interest beyond the statutory limits, or whether the lender has provided adequate notice regarding the foreclosure? These latter questions give the reader more meaningful insight into what to expect in the analysis portion of the memorandum.

Lastly, you must address the relevant facts. Only state the facts that have an impact on the issue to be analyzed. If you provide the reader with irrelevant facts, you demonstrate that you do not have the ability to discern which facts will assist you in addressing the issue. If you leave out significant facts, the reader is left to wonder if you know what facts need to be addressed in order to ultimately answer the legal question. Be sure that the facts are stated accurately and in an unbiased manner. The reader should have a basic understanding of the relevant facts, but still should be left wondering what will be the answer to the question posed. In an objective memorandum, stating the facts in a manner that clearly shows the reader the ultimate answer is incorrect. The document must take the reader step by step through your thought processes to get the answer to the legal question. At the place where you write the issue statement, we are simply acknowledging there is a viable legal question. After all, if the answer to the question were obvious, there would have been no reason to engage in writing a memorandum.

INCORRECT: Under Chapter 45 of the N.C. General Statutes, has a lender committed fraud when the lender intentionally misrepresented material facts to the homeowner?

Even without an understanding of the statutory requirements for fraud, it is fairly obvious that the lender has engaged in fraud. It is not clear that there was a viable question. We write memoranda when there are viable questions that need to be researched, analyzed and answered. Here, there were only facts presented that strongly suggest the lender has committed fraud. If these are the only facts, then there is really no issue. If you only have these one-sided facts with an obvious conclusion, you will need to reconsider if you have properly identified the issue.

CORRECT: Under Chapter 45 of the N.C. General Statutes, has a lender committed fraud when the lender orally advised the homeowner he had a fixed rate, but the written documents all stated the homeowner had an adjustable rate and the lender gave the homeowner an opportunity to review the documents before closing?

In this example, the reader is left with a viable question. On the one hand, the lender did tell the homeowner he was getting a fixed rate, but on the other hand, the documents stated different terms. The homeowner could have read the documents and discovered that he had an adjustable rate prior to the closing. Yet, the lender never corrected its oral representation with a new, accurate oral representation regarding the true nature of the interest rate. Is the lender protected since it gave the homeowner an opportunity to review the written documents? With these new facts, the reader is left to determine how you applied the statutory authority to answer this question. The answer is not obvious. The reader can anticipate what both sides will say. The lender will argue that it gave the homeowner the documents and the homeowner had a responsibility to read those documents. The homeowner will argue that it was reasonable to rely on the oral statements of the lender and he had no reason to anticipate that the documents would be substantially different from what the lender told him. When the reader can see the anticipated arguments in the issue statement, you have appropriately captured the facts.

There are two formats for the proper issue statement; "under... does... when? and "the issue is whether..."

EXAMPLES:

Under (this law), does (this legal question) when (these facts) are presented?

The issue is whether under (this law) is/would/can this legal question when (these facts) are presented.

Both formats require the same information. Either format will be appropriate for a memorandum or other legal document. However, it is preferable to avoid using them both interchangeably. In other words, if you use "under … does … when …" for the first issue statement, that same format should be used for all issue statements in that document. "Under … does … when …" is a question and should end with a question mark. "The issue is whether …" is a declarative sentence and should finish with a period.

Keys to outstanding issue statements:

Step 1: Be sure the statement is clear. There is a great amount of information that will be included in this statement. However, the overarching rules of clarity and precision in legal writing must still be met.

Step 2: Use numbering or categorizing to assist with clarity.

EXAMPLE:

The issue is whether under *State v. Jackson*, a defendant can be forced to take psychopathic drugs when: 1) the defendant signed a power of attorney appointing a guardian when she was in a lucid state; 2) the guardian has refused to agree to the treatment; 3) the guardian is a possible witness for the prosecution; and 4) the defendant has not waived the potential conflict of interest.

It may be easier to understand the facts if they are numbered. This technique may not be necessary if there are only a few succinct facts.

Step 3: Edit the statement for clarity. Even the most seasoned legal writers may not be able to write such a complex sentence with clarity and precision after the first attempt. The key is to be sure that the statement conveys everything you want it to convey in a manner that will be clear to a reader after only reading the statement once.

EXAMPLES
Example A

The issue is whether the foster parent is considered the most recent foster parent when the foster parent sends the foster child away to an eight-month program, where the child stays outside of the foster parent's home, the foster parent signs an assignment of parentage, and the child is sent to a foster care facility to stay and not to an individual foster parent.

Or

Under N.C. Gen. Stat 1906-5, does a foster parent continue to be treated as the most recent foster parent when the foster parent takes the foster child to an eight-month program where the child stays outside of the foster parent's home, the foster parent signs an assignment of parentage, and the foster child is sent to a foster care facility to stay and not to an individual foster parent?

Note that in the first example, the writer uses the name of the statute. In the second example, the writer uses the number of the statute. Either version will assist the reader in identifying the source of law that will be analyzed. The legal question is whether the foster parent is considered the most recent foster parent. Asking whether the foster parent gets to adopt the child would have been too broad to give the reader an idea of what was really to be addressed. The facts show there is a viable argument on both sides. The foster parent will argue that he is the most recent foster parent, because the child was not sent to another foster parent, but to a facility. A facility should not be considered a "parent." The opposing side will argue that the foster parent is not the most recent foster parent when the child was sent away for eight months. This is a fairly long period of time. Further, the foster parent signed an assignment of parentage. The purpose of that document was likely to relinquish the foster parent's responsibilities over to the facility. The reader has been presented with the law, the defined legal question, and enough facts to appreciate and anticipate the potential arguments.

Example B

The issue is whether the moral turpitude exception to the foster parent's exclusive right to adoption rule will apply when the foster parent engages in an openly homosexual relationship with a live-in boyfriend who stays in the home with the child, sleeps in the same bedroom with the boyfriend next to the child's bedroom, and kisses the boyfriend in front of the child.

Or

Under the moral turpitude exception to the foster parent's exclusive right to adoption rule, does the foster parent lose his exclusive right to adopt the child when the foster parent engages in an openly homosexual relationship with a live-in boyfriend who stays in the home with the child, sleeps in the same bedroom with the boyfriend next to the child's bedroom, and kisses the boyfriend in front of the child?

Here, the reader learns that the foster parent has the exclusive right to adopt a foster child unless that foster parent has violated the moral turpitude exception. This particular foster parent is in an openly gay relationship. The legal question is whether being in an openly gay relationship violates the moral turpitude exception. The foster dad will argue that he has not done anything inappropriate in the child's presence. Sharing a bed and kissing are ordinary acts that people in a relationship engage in. The party seeking to apply the moral turpitude exception will argue that it is inappropriate to have a live-in gay lover. Furthermore, sharing a bed with another man in the home where the child stays and kissing that man in front of the child are all inappropriate acts. The basic positions of both sides are reflected in the issue statements.

Example C

The issue is whether under N.C. Gen. Stat. § 75-1.3 [the Anti-Monopoly Act], Mary will be deemed to have monopolized the doughnut business in North Carolina where there are 100 doughnut shops in North Carolina, and she owns fifty of those shops. Mary is seeking to purchase twenty-five additional doughnut shops, giving her seventy-five doughnut shops in the state and making her the largest doughnut shop owner in the state. Mary has acquired her doughnut shops by running local proprietors out of business.

Or

Under N.C. Gen. Stat. § 75-1.3 [the Anti-Monopoly Act], can Mary be deemed to have monopolized the doughnut business in North Carolina when there are 100 doughnut shops in North Carolina; she owns fifty of the doughnut shops; she is seeking to purchase twenty-five additional doughnut shops from Bonnie, giving her seventy-five doughnut shops in the state (making her the largest doughnut shop owner in the state), and Mary has acquired her doughnut shops by running local business owners out of business?

Here, the writer has identified the law by the number of the statute or the name. The legal question is whether Mary has monopolized the doughnut business. The relevant facts are that she currently owns fifty shops and is seeking to purchase twenty-five more shops. She will be the largest doughnut shop owner in the area, and apparently she engages in aggressive business tactics. Mary will likely argue that being the biggest and most aggressive doughnut shop owner does not automatically mean she has a monopoly. Mary currently owns fifty, or one-half, of the doughnut shops in the state. Mary will argue half is not a monopoly. Further, if she acquires the additional twenty-five, she will only own seventy-five percent of the doughnut shops in the state. She will not own 100 percent of the doughnut shops. There will be twenty-five other doughnut shops that she does not own. On the other side, it will be argued that Mary has bullied her way into being the largest doughnut shop owner in the state. The anti-monopoly laws were designed to prevent such behavior. Owning seventy-five out of 100 shops is enough to consider her ownership a monopoly.

The issue is whether under the "exclusive benefit" exception to N.C. Gen. Stat. § 75-1.3 [the Anti-Monopoly Act] the Biscoe doughnut shop is for the exclusive benefit of minorities when the doughnut shop occasionally serves men and is in an all-female populated city, even though the city may be diversified due to the opening of a new factory, which may employ male workers.

Or

Under the "exclusive benefit" exception to the N.C. Gen. Stat. § 75-1.3 [the Anti-Monopoly Act], is the Biscoe doughnut shop for the exclusive benefit of minorities when the doughnut shop occasionally serves men and is in an all-female populated city, even though the city may be diversified due to the opening of a new factory, which may employ male workers?

The reader is made aware that there is an exception to the anti-monopoly rule when the business is for the exclusive benefit of minorities. Thus, it would be acceptable for Mary to have a monopoly if her business is exclusively benefiting minorities. The legal question is whether the exception applies to the doughnut shop in Biscoe, which is a city populated with only females. Mary would like for the exception to apply, so she will argue that the shop is in an all-female city, and females are minorities. The fact that the shop occasionally serves men is of no consequence because the shop is still located in an all-female city. The opposing side will point out that the shop cannot be for the "exclusive" benefit of women when it serves men. Furthermore, there is a strong likelihood that the shop will begin to serve more men because a new factory is opening in the city and it will hire male workers. The male workers will likely go to the doughnut shop, increasing the number of male patrons and taking away any exclusive usage the all-female city had on the shop. The reader will have to look to the analysis section of the document to learn how "exclusive" has been interpreted.

Example D

Under the North Carolina Anti-Predatory Lending law [N.C. Gen. Stat. § 24-2], is Dee considered the borrower when she is the sole heiress to her mother's estate, and her mother owned a one-half interest in her home and her mother's home was encumbered by a mortgage, but her mother never signed the promissory note?

Or

The issue is whether under the North Carolina Anti-Predatory Lending law [N.C. Gen. Stat. § 24-2 et seq.] Dee is considered the borrower when she is the sole heiress to her mother's estate, and her mother owned a one-half interest in her home and her mother's home was encumbered by a mortgage, but her mother never signed the promissory note.

Example E

Under the North Carolina Anti-Predatory Lending law [N.C. Gen. Stat. § 24-10.2 et seq.], did Cee (the co-owner) receive a benefit from the loan transaction when: (1) she had a $15,000.00 mortgage on the property that was two months behind; (2) the loan paid her 2006 property taxes; (3) her $1,500.00 credit card bill was paid; (4) she received a stove; (5) the original loan had a fixed interest rate; (6) the new loan had an adjustable rate; and (7) the actual borrower received $59,000.00?

Or

The issue is whether under North Carolina Anti-Predatory Lending law [N.C. Gen. Stat. § 24-10.2 et seq.] Cee (the co-owner) received a benefit from the loan transaction when: (1) she had a $15,000.00 mortgage on the property that was two months behind; (2) the loan paid her 2006 property taxes; (3) her $1,500.00 credit card bill was paid; (4) she received a stove; (5) the original loan had a fixed interest rate; (6) the new loan had an adjustable rate; and (7) the actual borrower received $59,000.00.

CHAPTER 5

✝

STATUTORY INTERPRETATION

S tate and national legislatures make laws, including statutes. Ordinances are made by local governments. Regulations are promulgated by administrative agencies. State constitutions usually involve a combination of legislature and voters' actions. The function of statutes is to: (1) regulate categories of persons, events, or things; and (2) solve broad problems in society.

Under the constitutional doctrine of separation of powers, the judiciary is equal to the legislative branch of government, but separate. Courts resolve controversies between specific parties involving the specific individuals and events in litigation. The courts apply the details of disputes to statutes for resolution. Occasionally, if a statute's language is vague or ambiguous, the court must engage in statutory interpretation in order to try to follow the meaning of the statute. The courts NEVER rewrite statutes or second guess the legislature's intent. They do not have the same power over statutes as compared to case law, where courts can overrule or modify cases. A statute remains fixed unless it is changed or abolished by the legislature or declared unconstitutional by a court. While courts can, and do, interpret the meaning and application of a statute, they cannot amend its language or any unambiguous meaning.

The role of attorneys in statutory interpretation is to ethically guide the court's application of a statute to the client's case. Attorneys should construct arguments favorable to the client's case, as long as the interpretation is made in good faith.

There are several types of interpretation. You may only be looking at a single statute. You might be comparing a statute to another. There may be a question as to whether a statute is invalid because it violates the constitution or whether a regulation is invalid because it is beyond the scope of a statute. A statute may change a common law doctrine. In each scenario, a different method of statutory interpretation is used.

THE PROCESS OF ANALYZING THE STATUTE

Sometimes the law is not precise as to how it may relate to a certain fact pattern or issue. Where the statute is vague or ambiguous, you must engage in statutory interpretation to decipher the meaning of the law and how it relates to your facts. In order to engage in statutory interpretation, you should first locate the applicable statute. Determine whether you have the version in effect at the time the cause of action arose. Read the entire statute and mark the sections that address your facts. Read the statute, looking carefully at the language. Identify conjunctives, disjunctives, discretionary, and mandatory language. Identify relationships among the elements. Look for statutory definitions. When the same language is used throughout the act, the language is assumed to have the same meaning in the act. Read all preliminary and prefatory information and any notes or comments following the statute. Outline the elements or requirements of the statute. Identify your statutory issues and draft a preliminary issue statement. Lastly, apply statutory rules or canons of construction. If necessary, research the paper trail of a bill as it works its way through the different stages of the legislative process. Sources of legislative history include the original written bill, transcripts of hearings on the bill, committee reports, proposed amendments and debates.

The primary skills here are recognizing statutory ambiguity and applying the canons of statutory construction. In other words, we are still identifying issues and key facts. We extend the analysis by applying rules to the language of the governing statute. There are several methods of statutory interpretation: (a) the Plain Meaning Rule; (b) the Mischief Rule; (c) the Golden Rule; (d) *Expressio Unius Est Exclusio Alterius*; (e) *Noscitur a Sociis*; (f) *Ejusdem Generis*; (g) *In Pari Materia*; (h) Terms of Art; (i) Strict Construction; and (j) Liberal Construction.

Pay attention to the *stare decisis* doctrine and precedent discussed previously in Chapter Two. Remember that a court's interpretation becomes precedent that other courts within the jurisdiction must follow. Apply each part, element, or definition in a statute to the facts of your case. If a court has previously interpreted the language or application of a statute, apply that interpretation to the facts in your client's case.

The canons of statutory interpretation are defined below:

Plain Meaning Rule: If the language of a statute has a plain meaning, it must be followed. If there is no ambiguity within the four corners of the text, the court's sole function is to enforce the statute according to its terms.

Mischief Rule: A statute is to be read in light of some assumed purpose or objective. Every law should be construed, if possible, to give effect to all its provisions. In addition, when words of a law in their application to an existing situation are clear and free from all ambiguity, the letter of the law shall not be disregarded under the pretense of pursuing the spirit of law.

Golden Rule: Do not follow the literal meaning of a statute when the literal reading would produce absurd results.

Expressio Unius Est Exclusio Alterius: "The expression of one thing is the exclusion of another." When a writer specifically mentions one item, he or she by implication intends to exclude some other item.

Noscitur a Sociis: "It is known from its associates." The meaning of a word is or may be known from the accompanying words. Words in a sentence can have meaning because of their association with other words in a sentence or paragraph. This canon cautions against taking words out of context.

Ejusdem Generis: "Of the same kind." A general, catch-all phrase is limited in meaning to the same category or classification found within the specific items in the preceding list.

In Pari Materia: "On the same subject." Statutes on the same subject are to be interpreted together even though they may have been passed at different times. While there may be differences between the statutes, courts will attempt to interpret them as consistent with each other. However, when statutes are inconsistent, then the more recent or more particular statute will usually control over the earlier or more general statute.

Terms of Art: Words and phrases having a special or technical meaning are called terms of art. Statutory language is to be interpreted according to the ordinary meaning of the words unless it is clear that the legislature intended a different meaning.

Strict Construction: The narrow reading of the statutory language. Under strict construction, a court would prefer a narrow or less inclusive interpretation of the language.

Liberal Construction: The broad reading of the statutory language. Under liberal construction, a court would prefer a broader or more inclusive interpretation of the language.

Consider the following examples. Which canon of statutory interpretation would best decipher the legislative intent behind the rule?

Example A

§ 1A-1, Rule 20: Joinder. Multiple plaintiffs may join in a single civil action where they assert any right to relief jointly, severally, or in the alternative in respect of or arising out of the same transaction, occurrence, or series of transactions or occurrences and if any question of law or fact common to all parties will arise in the action. The purpose of this rule is to promote trial convenience and expedite the final determination of disputes, thereby preventing multiple lawsuits.

§ 1D-25(b): Punitive damages awarded against a defendant shall not exceed three times the amount of compensatory damages or two hundred fifty thousand dollars ($250,000.00), whichever is greater. If a trier of fact returns a verdict for punitive damages in excess of the maximum amount specified under this subsection, the trial court shall reduce the award and enter judgment for punitive damages in the maximum amount.

A corporate defendant argues that the punitive damages cap applies per defendant, not per plaintiff, in a case where two plaintiffs consolidated their claims. The defendant argues that it cannot be ordered to pay more than $250,000.00 total. The plaintiffs argue that the defendant must pay $250,000.00 per plaintiff, totaling $500,000.00. How should the court rule based on the above statute?

The defendant's interpretation of section 1D-25(b) would surely result in an absurd consequence. In contravention of the court's history of promoting judicial economy, savvy plaintiffs will surely be encouraged to bring multiple lawsuits if the court adopted the defendant's construction by isolating one particular portion of section 1D-25(b) (that "punitive damages awarded against a defendant shall not exceed" the amount specified therein). Such a result would directly contradict the purpose behind the rules regarding joinder of parties. The court should not read segments of a statute in isolation. Rather, sections 1A-1, Rule 20 and 1D-25(b) should be construed *in pari materia*, giving effect to every provision. The court should interpret section 1D-25(b) as such to enter judgment ordering the defendant to pay a total of $500,000.00.

Example B

§ 31B(1). Right to Renounce Succession. A person who succeeds to a property interest as

1. Heir; or
2. Next of kin; or
3. evisee; or
4. Legatee; or
5. Beneficiary of a life insurance policy who did not possess the incidents of ownership under the policy at the time of death of the insured; or
6. Person succeeding to a renounced interest; or
7. Beneficiary under a testamentary trust or under an *inter vivos* trust; or
8. Appointee under a power of appointment exercised by a testamentary instrument or a nontestamentary instrument; or
9. Surviving joint tenant, surviving tenant by the entireties, or surviving tenant of a tenancy with a right of survivorship; or may renounce at any time, in whole or in part, the right of succession to any property or interest therein, including a future interest, by filing a written instrument under the provisions of this Chapter.

A mother sues herself for the wrongful death of her seven year-old son after she allowed him to ride on the hood of the car. When he fell off, the car, operated by the mother, rolled over him. The mother admitted that she could not recover damages. She renounced her right to damages as the boy's sole heir to the benefit of her daughters, the deceased's sisters. Can this action be maintained?

Under section 31B-1, the only entities who can renounce an interest in property are the listed capacities. The list does not include beneficiaries of wrongful death recoveries. Under the doctrine of *expressio unius est exclusio alterius*, when a statute lists the situations to which it applies, it implies the exclusion of situations not contained in the list. The purpose of the renunciation statute is to provide according to its terms for renunciation of property interests which are transferred by intestate succession or by wills, life insurance, testamentary or inter vivos trusts, pension plans, or other such voluntarily drawn instruments of transfer. The legislature did not intend the statute to apply to recoveries under the Wrongful Death Act.

Example C

§ 90-21.13(b) Informed Consent for Medical Treatment: A consent which is evidenced in writing and which is signed by the patient or other authorized person, shall be presumed to be a valid consent. This presumption, however, may be subject to rebuttal only upon proof that such consent was obtained by fraud, deception or misrepresentation of a material fact.

An injured patient sues a hospital, arguing that he did not consent to a certain procedure. His argument is that his signature, although not procured through actual misrepresentation, was procured through negligent misrepresentation. Does this situation fall under the statute?

Standing alone, the term "misrepresentation" appears broad enough to encompass negligent misrepresentation; however, as the last in the series "fraud, deception or misrepresentation," the principle of *ejusdem generis* indicates that only knowing and intentional behavior is intended. Therefore, the patient should not be able to make a successful argument for negligent misrepresentation.

Remember, the key in statutory interpretation is to analyze a statute to discover if the textual meaning is ambiguous or vague. Use all available tools. Construct arguments on both sides of the issue. Predict which arguments are most persuasive.

Tips to Remember Statutory Canons of Interpretation

1. The big three: The Plain Meaning Rule—just follow the language. The Mischief Rule versus the Golden Rule—these are very close, but if a particular construction of a statute makes you chuckle because it's so ridiculous, the appropriate rule is the Golden Rule. Otherwise, the Mischief Rule will probably be more applicable.

2. Our Latin Maxims/Canons

   a. *In pari materia*. If you are ever asked to construe a particular statute in light of another, the correct maxim to use is *in pari materia*.

   b. *Ejusdem generis* vs. *expressio unius est exclusio alterius* vs. *noscitur a sociis*. Your first indicator that one of these maxims is to be used is a list of items. If the list ends in some general or generic term, e.g., coats, hats, umbrellas, or other personal items—the correct maxim to use will most probably be *ejusdem generis*.

   c. *Ejusdem generis* vs. *expressio unius est exclusio alterius* vs. *noscitur a sociis*. To remember *expressio unius est exclusio alterius*, simply remember that *expressio* means expression, *unius* (or *uno*) means one, *est* means is, *exclusio* means exclusion, and *alterius* means the alternative. You do not have to be a Latin scholar to break this one apart to see that the expression of one thing means the implied exclusion of another.

   d. The same can be done with *noscitur a sociis*. *Noscitur* sounds suspiciously like the word "know." *Sociis* is also suspiciously close to the word "associates." Together, you immediately know that the term means "to know something by its associates."

Statutory Interpretation Exercise

Your client, Ms. Turner, has presented you with the following facts: Mr. Walker was traveling to his mother's home for Thanksgiving dinner. He was driving about five miles over the speed limit. As he got closer to his mother's house, the road became curvier.

Normally, Mr. Walker would continue to speed because he had a sports car and he liked taking curves in that vehicle. However, on this Thanksgiving, Mr. Walker was driving his sports utility vehicle. Consequently, when he got to the curved turns, he slowed down to about ten miles under the speed limit, knowing that his SUV could not take the curves like his sports car could. As he was driving, Mr. Walker struck Ms. Turner, who was coming from the opposite direction. She was injured. She wants you to file a personal injury claim against Mr. Walker based on negligent and reckless driving. However, knowing that Mr. Walker was not speeding, you need to interpret the speeding statute to determine whether it will harm the case. Accordingly, your issue to research is whether there is a defense against speeding if one drives below the speed limit.

The pertinent statute is N.C. Gen. Stat. § 20-141. Speed restrictions:

a. No person shall drive a vehicle on a highway or in a public vehicular area at a speed greater than is reasonable and prudent under the conditions then existing.

b. Except as otherwise provided in this Chapter, it shall be unlawful to operate a vehicle in excess of the following speeds:

(1) Thirty-five miles per hour inside municipal corporate limits for all vehicles.

(2) Fifty-five miles per hour outside municipal corporate limits for all vehicles except for school buses and school activity buses.

c. The fact that the speed of a vehicle is lower than the foregoing limits shall not relieve the operator of a vehicle from the duty to decrease speed as may be necessary to avoid colliding with any person, vehicle or other conveyance on or entering the highway, and to avoid injury to any person or property.

1. You believe that a strict reading of the statute is incorrect because such a reading would lead to an erroneous conclusion. Using the Golden Rule, draft an argument that Mr. Walker would not have a defense under section 20-141(c).

2. You believe that Mr. Walker's counsel would use the Plain Meaning Rule to make an argument against that Mr. Walker could not have been negligent because he was obeying all traffic laws at the time of the collision. Using this rule, draft an argument that opposing counsel could use against your client in this action.

Suggested Response

Mr. Walker's literal interpretation of section 20-141(c) is erroneous. Where a literal interpretation would contravene a statute's manifest purpose, the strict letter of the statute should be disregarded. Even more specifically here, sections and subsections must be construed as a whole and in a manner that gives effect to the reason and purpose of the statute. Additionally, statutes imposing criminal liability must be strictly construed so that the scope of the statute may not be extended by implication to include offenses not clearly made illegal.

Applying those rules, section 20-141(c) should only impose liability on a motorist whose failure to reduce speed to avoid a collision is not in keeping with the duty to use due care under the circumstances. The obvious purpose of section 20-141 is to authorize specific speed limits and to establish a duty for all motorists to use due care in maintaining the speed of their vehicle. The statute must be construed consistent with subsection (a)'s requirement that no person shall drive at a speed greater than is reasonable and prudent under the circumstances. Section 20-141(c) does not impose liability except in cases where a reasonable and ordinarily prudent person could, and would have, decreased his speed to avoid a collision. Interpreting the statute otherwise is contrary to well-established rules of statutory construction and achieves strained, unreasonable, and wholly unintended results.

The fact that the speed of a vehicle is lower than the foregoing limits should not relieve the driver from the duty to decrease speed when approaching and going around a curve to avoid causing injury to any person or property either on or off the highway, in compliance with legal requirements and the duty of all persons to use due care.

CHAPTER 6

✝

CASE LAW ANALYSIS

Here is the promised land of the law, where you begin to discuss the cases to establish the basis for your legal conclusions. Case law analysis is a methodical approach to a discussion of case precedent. Always be careful in the manner you reference the dispute. If you are analyzing a matter before litigation has been filed, do not reference it as a case. Often the clients come to you in anticipation of possible litigation. It would be inappropriate to refer to the parties as "plaintiff" and "defendant" when no case has been filed. If a case has been filed, you should refer to it as "the case" or "the case at bar," but if this is a pre-litigation matter, you should refer to the "situation," "matter," "dispute," or another appropriate term. Similarly, on appeal, the parties will be appellants and appellees. In a will caveat proceeding, the parties are propounders and caveators.

Remember that you are constrained by *stare decisis*, as discussed in Chapter Two. Ethics rules will also dictate some limitations on your treatment of the cases when you present the research to the court. If there is a case that is practically the same as your case (known as "on all fours"), you cannot ignore that case, even if it is not helpful. You will need to acknowledge it and attempt, as best you can, to distinguish it from your dispute. If you are discussing the case precedent, you cannot omit significant analogies and distinctions if the result is that your portrayal of the case is no longer accurate. Making legal arguments is not the same as misrepresenting the law. The art of the legal argument comes into play when you are finding clever analogies and distinctions and explaining how much weight each should be afforded. Even an interoffice memorandum should have fair treatment of the cases. You cannot take the "ostrich" approach and hide your head in the sand to avoid damaging precedent cases. You adjust your strategy and your theory to respond to the research.

Precedent

First, you must decide which case precedent to use. Court opinions have been recorded in some form since the inception of the American legal system. It is not accurate to state that courts never contradict themselves. After all, courts have changed over the years. Generally new judges are elected for six- to eight-year terms. Judges retire or lose elections, and new judges are elected or appointed. The new judge on the bench is not completely confined by the ruling of previous judges. The weight of the case precedent varies based on the court the judge sits on. For example, under no circumstances can a judge on a lower court overrule the precedent established by a higher court. In North Carolina, the Court of Appeals is a lower court than the Supreme Court. Precedent set by the Court of Appeals can be overturned by the Supreme Court. However, the N.C. Court of Appeals has no authority to overturn any precedent set by the N.C. Supreme Court.

As a legal analyst, you are bound by any mandatory authority in your jurisdiction. When dealing with a state law matter in North Carolina, you are bound by the cases decided by the North Carolina Court of Appeals, North Carolina Supreme Court, and the United States Supreme Court. If you are addressing a federal law matter in North Carolina, you are bound by the Fourth Circuit Court of Appeals and the United States Supreme Court.

If there is case law that does not fall under mandatory authority, it may be utilized as persuasive authority. Persuasive authority is case law that the court does not have to follow. For example, if you are in the Fourth Circuit Court of Appeals and there was a very helpful case that was decided by the Fifth Circuit Court of Appeals, you may reference this case. The Fourth Circuit Court of Appeals is of equal authority as the Fifth Circuit Court of Appeals, but only in the jurisdictions it covers. Thus, the Fourth Circuit Court of Appeals can consider other jurisdictions' opinions, but it is not bound to follow them.

You should always use precedent when you have adequate precedential authority. You should only use persuasive authority when there is a lack of helpful mandatory authority. Unfortunately, it is a sign of weakness in your case when you must heavily rely on the persuasive authority.

Once you have selected cases to use in your analysis, you can begin the actual case law analysis. The following steps need to be completed in each case that you are analyzing. There will come a point later in your document where you will compare and contrast the cases with each other. However, at the beginning of the analysis, you need to develop the precedential cases individually so the discussion is clear.

Step 1. State the facts of the precedent case. You must begin the case analysis by explaining what happened in the precedential case. A full recitation of the facts is not necessary. Provide the reader with enough facts to give the case context. Make sure you also include the facts that will impact the legal analysis. Never address any comparison and contrasts of the precedent cases and the present situation without fully explaining the facts in the precedent cases. Remember, you are writing to a reader who may not be familiar with the case precedent. You can never assume that your readers have read the case or are familiar with the case. Even if the readers know the precedent, they may not have gleaned the appropriate facts that you will expound upon in your analysis.

Step 2. State the holding of the precedential case. Now that you have explained the case facts, tell the reader what the court held. In properly stating the holding, remember that you should say "the court held…" It is inappropriate to state that "the court felt…" or "the court thought…" etc. In judicial opinions, courts "find" facts and "hold" rulings.

Example: The court found that the plaintiff had not engaged in any act of contributory negligence. The court held that the defendant was liable for the damages to the plaintiff's truck.

Step 3. State the rationale for the holding of the precedential case. In a brief and clear manner, explain the court's ruling. Stating the court's ruling without giving an explanation of it greatly weakens the effectiveness of the position you are seeking to further in your analysis. Steps 2 and 3 can be combined.

Example: The court held that the defendant was liable for the damages to the plaintiff's truck because the plaintiff presented evidence that the defendant hit the plaintiff's truck after running a red light.

Step 4. State the analogies between the precedent case and the present situation. Now that you have presented the precedential case's facts, holding, and rationale, you can explain how the case precedent provides a predictive factor for the outcome of the present situation. The predictive factor is based on the strength of the analogies and distinctions between the precedent and the present situation. When there are very strong analogies, there is a very strong likelihood that the court will rule the same in the present situation.

Be sure to only note the *relevant* analogies and distinctions. Stating generic and irrelevant analogies does not further your analysis. Your goal is not to create the longest list of analogies. Instead, your goal should be to establish whether the case precedent and the present situation are similar, justifying the similar treatment of the two matters. Some analogies are irrelevant and do not further your argument. Avoid mentioning analogies such as the following:

Incorrect: In both cases, there was a defendant who was charged with a crime.

This is true in all felony cases and does not ultimately further any significant point.

Incorrect: In both cases, the plaintiff demanded money damages.

This is true in all civil cases. A writer who states such generic analogies is generally not clear on the facts that will ultimately impact the analysis. Throwing in the "kitchen sink" is not a concept that effectively works here. In law school, there are page limits imposed to encourage the students to make judgment calls on what facts are irrelevant. In practice, local rules also have page limits imposed, but more importantly, there is the loss of credibility for the attorney who does not figure out which analogies to include.

Correct examples: In both cases, the person who took out the loan received a large cash payment.

In both cases, the adjustable interest rates on the new loans resulted in higher interest rates than the homeowners would have had with the old loans.

Step 5. State the distinctions between the precedent case and the present situation. The distinctions are equally as important as the analogies. If the case precedent has many significant distinctions from the present situation, there will be a strong likelihood that the court will not rule similarly. For clarity, state the distinctions in two separate sentences.

Example: In *McAllister*, the borrower had an adjustable rate on the original loan. In the present case, Cee had a fixed interest rate.

Example: In *Wally*, Ms. Wally owned the home at the time of the refinance. In the present case, Dee did not own the home at the time of the refinance, but inherited her interest later.
Only the distinctions that impact the analysis need to be addressed. Avoid the following type of distinctions:

Examples: In *Case A*, the plaintiff was seeking $10,000.00. In *Case B*, the plaintiff was seeking $10,500.00.
While these facts are likely true, if the $500.00 difference does not impact the analysis, you have wasted valuable space on your document and wasted the reader's time. If you find that there are not correlative facts on both sides, this is often a sign that this is not a relevant distinction.

Example: In *Case A*, the defendant refused to take the breathalyzer. In *Case B*, there is no evidence whether the defendant took the breathalyzer or not.

There is a strong likelihood that the use of the breathalyzer will not be a key issue in the analysis because the usage of the breathalyzer was not addressed at all in *Case B*.

Step 6. State the significance of the analogies and distinctions. This last step is critical, because the reader needs to understand how much weight you have given the analogies and distinctions. There will be times when the number of analogies and distinctions do not reflect the prediction you are making for the outcome of the present situation. There may be a larger number of analogies, but the distinctions are so significant that you have determined the court will not likely rule as it did in the case precedent. This is the information that the readers need you to explain based on your reading of the cases.

Keys to a Great Analysis

The facts in the case precedent occurred in the past. Use past tense verbs in your discussion.

Avoid discussing multiple analogies or distinctions at one time. Address them individually.

CHAPTER 7

✝

SYNTHESIS

Synthesis is the binding together of several decisions into a whole that stands for a rule or a general legal principle. By focusing on the reasoning and general facts that the cases have in common, synthesis finds and explains collective meaning that is not apparent from the individual cases themselves. In other words, you will read the cases collectively to determine what they are saying as a whole. During synthesis, you will blend the holdings of several cases into a single general principle or rule.

Synthesis is NOT a mere description of several cases, one after another. It is not a synthesis to describe Case A, describe Case B, describe Case C, and then stop. You need to do more to tie it all together. It is always helpful to use a chart rather than an outline. Study the following steps:

Case	A	B	C
Facts	D ignores a sign warning trespassers to keep out and enters P's land to smell his award-winning roses.	D ignores a sign warning trespassers to keep out and enters P's land, seeking to escape a herd of stampeding cattle.	D ignores a sign warning trespassers to keep out and enters P's land, seeking to escape a herd of stampeding cattle. While evading the cattle, D accidentally tramples on P's award-winning roses.
Holding	Held: D is liable for trespass.	Held: D is not liable for trespass.	Held: D is liable for damages to P's roses.

Determine the general principle (or rule statement) that we derive from synthesizing these three cases. The general principle is: A person who enters the land of another without permission is liable for trespass, except where entry is necessary to avoid physical danger, in which case a person is liable only for actual damage to the property.

Synthesis is the process by which we harmonize cases to develop a rule, exceptions, and limitations.

The Process

Before you do any writing, (1) research; (2) group cases together according to holdings; (3) note factual similarities (key or determinative facts); (4) note factual distinctions (key or determinative facts); and (5) determine the general principles. Look at the following examples of cases involving warrantless searches.

The general principle from Cases 1, 2, and 5: Where a search without a warrant takes place in an individual's private residence, the court is more likely to hold that the search violated the person's reasonable expectation of privacy under the Fourth Amendment. Moreover, the nature of the entry does not appear to have any bearing on the outcome. The result was the same whether the police forced their way into the home or whether they were admitted without force.

The general principle in Cases 3 and 4: Where a search without a warrant occurs in a public place, the court is less likely to hold the search violated the individual's reasonable expectation of privacy under the Fourth Amendment. Moreover, where a suspect's home is involved, some type of actual intrusion into the private residence would appear to be required.

The general principle from all cases is: The courts are more likely to hold that one's right to a reasonable expectation of privacy under the Fourth Amendment has been violated where a search without a warrant occurs in a private residence, as opposed to a public location. This is true regardless of whether entry into the private residence was forced. However, some type of physical or actual entry is required.

Now that you have determined the general principle, it is time to write the synthesis. You will need to follow these steps: (a) formulate an opening statement; (b) discuss the cases; and (c) arrive at a conclusion.

The Opening Statement includes the common features or general principles of the cases, noting any exceptions or limitations.

The discussion of the cases should occur individually and with reference to one another. Include key facts with analogies and distinctions. Note the causes of action, issues raised, reasoning of courts, holdings of courts, and resulting rules (formulated, applied, expanded, narrowed, or overturned) from your cases.

Conclude.

Example: Read and take notes regarding the cases you are synthesizing. Assume that all of the following cases were decided in the jurisdiction of Kent, where the age of majority is 18.

Case One: *Green v. Green*, 1995

Jack Green sued his father Joseph for *negligently* pouring hot liquids in the kitchen so that he burned Jack in the process. Jack is 12 years old. HELD: Mr. Joseph Green is immune from suit.

Case Two: *Black v. Black*, 1998

Jamie Black sued her father Paul for battery, an *intentional tort*. Paul knocked Jamie's baseball cap off her head because Jamie struck out in the last inning of a Little League game. Jamie is ten years old. HELD: Mr. Paul Black is not immune from suit.

Case Three: *Brown v. Brown*, 2002

Joan Brown sued her mother Susan for assault, an *intentional tort,* for brandishing a tennis racket at her after she lost her serve in the final set of the women's twenty-five-and-under local tennis tournament. Joan is 24 years old and lives at home. HELD: Ms. Susan Brown is not immune from suit.

Case Four: *White v. White*, 2009

George sued his father Walter for *negligently* burning him in Walter White's kitchen by handing him a large hot pot. George is a 24-year-old businessman and is married. HELD: Mr. Walter White is not immune from suit.

Start with a blank synthesis chart.

Case				
Facts				
Objectives				
Legal Theories				
Issues				
Holdings				
Reasoning				

Fill in your chart case by case.

Case	Green	Black	Brown	White
Facts	A 12-year-old burned by hot liquids being poured by parent; sued parent for negligence.	A 10-year-old sued parent for battery for knocking her baseball cap off because she struck out during a game.	A 24-year-old sued her parent for assault for brandishing a tennis racket at her after she lost her serve in a tennis match.	A 24-year-old sued his parent for negligence after he was burned when his father handed him a large hot pot.
Objectives	Child: Recover damages for negligence. Parent: Avoid paying damages.	Child: Recover damages for intentional tort. Parent: Avoid paying damages.	Child: Recover damages for intentional tort. Parent: Avoid paying damages.	Child: Recover damages for negligence. Parent: Avoid paying damages.
Legal Theories	Child: Negligence. Parent: Immunity.	Child: Intentional tort. Parent: Immunity.	Child: Intentional tort. Parent: Immunity.	Child: Negligence Parent: Immunity.
Issues	Is a parent immune from suit by a minor child who was injured as a result of parent's negligence?	Is a parent immune from suit by a minor child who was injured as a result of being intention-ally struck by a parent?	Is a parent immune from suit by an adult child who was assaulted by the parent?	Is a parent immune from suit by an adult child who was injured as a result of the parent's negligence?
Holdings	YES	NO	NO	NO
Reasoning				

Synthesis: Here, two factors determine parental immunity from a tort suit in Kent: the type of tort involved, and the age of the child.

Example A

The courts have held that parents are immune from a negligence suit brought by their child. In *Green v. Green*, the father was held to be immune from a suit brought by his son where the father negligently burned him while pouring a hot liquid. The son in that case was 12 years old.

However, the courts have not held parents to be immune where an intentional tort is involved. For example, in *Brown v. Brown*, where a mother brandished a tennis racket at her 24-year-old daughter for losing her serve in a tennis match, the court held that the mother was not immune from the daughter's suit for assault. The court also held in *Black v. Black*, where a father knocked his daughter's baseball cap off because she struck out in the last inning of a Little League game, that the father was not immune from a suit for battery.

Moreover, where the court has upheld parental immunity for negligence, it has only done so where the suit is brought by a minor child. In *White v. White*, the court held that the parent was not immune from a 24-year-old son's suit for negligence.

The above cases define the scope of parental immunity in Kent. First, immunity extends to suits for negligence only. Parents are not immune from suits for intentional torts. Second, parents are not immune from a tort action that is brought by a child who is of majority age.

Example B

In *Green v. Green*, the court held that a parent was immune from a tort suit brought by his child. In that case, the parent negligently burned his 12-year-old son with a hot liquid. In a later case, *Black v. Black*, the court held that a parent was not immune from a tort suit brought by his child, where the parent knocked his child's baseball cap off after the child struck out in a Little League game. *Black v. Black* can be distinguished from *Green v. Green* in that *Green* involved an intentional tort. In *Brown v. Brown*, the court also held that a parent was not immune from a tort suit where the parent was sued for assault by her daughter for brandishing a tennis racket at the daughter when she lost her serve in a tennis match. This case is likewise distinguishable from *Green v. Green* in that it also involved an intentional tort.

Although the court held in *White v. White* that a parent was not immune from a tort suit brought by his son, where the parent negligently burned the son, that case can be distinguished from *Green v. Green*, in that the son in *White* was 24 years old, while the child in *Green* was 12.

The above cases define the scope of parental liability in Kent as follows: parental immunity extends to suits for negligence only. Parents are not immune from suits for intentional torts. Moreover, parents are not immune from tort actions that are brought by a child who is not a minor.

Remember, in synthesizing, one size does not fit all. You can only learn how to synthesize by doing it. Do not worry—synthesizing gets easier with practice

CHAPTER 8

✝

OBJECTIVE MEMORANDA

THE PURPOSE

In writing an interoffice memorandum, remember that the purpose of the document is to explain to the reader the relevant law regarding a case. You will be given a fact pattern (or the clients will tell you their story). You will either need to find relevant research or statutory and/or case law will be supplied to you. The objective memorandum is usually written for a busy supervisor, who needs a quick summary of how the law will treat the client's facts. Think of writing the memorandum as acting as the supervisor's brain—researching, analyzing, and forming conclusions, so she does not have to do so. The goal is to inform the reader. Your format should be predictive and objective. You should look at the facts you receive; apply the law to those facts and predict, as best you can, what you think will happen in the scenario provided to you based on that law.

Remember that you are not trying to convince or persuade anyone in an objective memorandum. You should not advocate one position over the other, even though you know your client's position. Your job is solely to explain the law and give an impression of what you believe the court will decide based on the applicable law. This memorandum will decide what the firm will do with this case, so analogies and distinctions are necessary where applicable. Feel free to use legal terms since you are corresponding with another lawyer, but do not use burdensome phrases.

The Format

The structure of a memorandum is simple. There should be a heading, introduction, brief answer, fact summary, rule(s) statement, discussion, and conclusion. Your heading should look like this:

To:

From:

Date:

Re:

No letterhead is needed because this document is used intra-office. If it will later be presented to another party, letterhead will be needed at that time. If it will later be filed in a court, an appropriate caption is necessary.

The introduction should include background information. An issue statement should immediately follow, focusing the reader (and the writer) on the important parts of your case. If there is more than one issue in the case, there should be more than one issue statement. There should always be a corresponding issue statement for every issue. Do not combine issues or issue statements, because that will defeat the entire purpose of the memorandum's organization. The issue(s) may also be presented in a question format. (See Chapter Four on Issue Formulation.) For the reader, the issue statement precisely refines the question presented. For the writer, it forces you to think carefully about the question to be decided and the key facts needed to answer that question.

Your brief answer should be just that—brief. Keep it concise, perhaps two to four sentences per issue. Cover the basics, including your impression of how the court will *likely* treat this set of facts and the general rules. There is no need to cite to cases or quote statutes here. The brief answer should address the same issues in the issue statements in the same order. The first sentence of the brief answer should answer the overall question.

Your fact summary should discuss the key facts of the case. Give a summary of facts that led the client to your office. For clarity, tell the story in chronological order. You must include every fact that you will mention in the discussion portion of the memo, but remember to only include background facts, and facts that will be discussed in the analysis section of the memo. Note that there are three types of facts: legally significant facts, emotionally significant facts, and background facts. Some must be included because they are essential. Some facts should be included because they are helpful. Remember to primarily use legally significant facts. For example, in an employment law case, a significant fact would be that the plaintiff and the defendant work in the same office for the same supervisor. It is legally insignificant that the plaintiff and defendant both drive red cars.

State the applicable statutes and case law. Use transitions; do not just list the rules you plan to use. Begin your discussion with the statute (if given) or case law that interprets the statute. Analogize case law similar to our facts. You will also need to distinguish cases that are not factually similar, even though the case is on the same topic. Your analysis and synthesis of the law involves applying the rule to your facts. Use the **CRAC** structure:

1. **C**onclusion
2. **R**ule
3. **A**nalysis

      a. case facts
      b. case holding
      c. rationale for the case holding
      d. analogies
      e. distinctions
      f. synthesis
      g. mini-conclusion

4. **C**onclusion

State the conclusion up front, followed by the rule or legal principle. Explain the elements required for a *prima facie* case or factors to weigh. Use case precedent and your facts to analogize and distinguish your facts and work your way to a conclusion. Do not waffle. For example, if your facts concern the revocation of a will, an effective rule section will read as follows:

> B.C.G.S. § 31-5.1(2) provides that "A written will, or any part thereof, may be revoked only… "[b]y being burnt, torn, canceled, obliterated, or destroyed, with the intent and for the purpose of revoking it, by the testator himself or by another person in his presence and by his direction." B.C.G.S. § 31-5.1(2) (2003). To be effective, revocation using any of the methods prescribed by G.S. 31-5.1(2), two things are necessary: (1) the doing of one of the acts specified under the statute, (2) accompanied by the present intent to revoke. *Thompson v. Royall*, 163 Va. 492 (1943); *In re Hodgin's Will*, 10 N.C. App. 492 (1971). In *White v. Casten*, the North Carolina Supreme Court noted that the act, whether by burning, tearing, or canceling, is a symbol of the testator's intent to revoke. 46 N.C. 197 (1853).

Note that this Rule section is a synthesis of statutory law and case law, organized from the more general to the more specific. In fact, the case law actually explains the statute. You will next give the facts and holdings of each case.

Example:

In *White v. Casten*, the North Carolina Supreme Court addressed the issue of whether a testator effectively revoked his will by burning. 46 N.C. 197 (1853). In that case, ...

In *Thompson v. Royall*, the testatrix purported to revoke her will by writing notations across the back of her will and codicil. 153 Va. 492. The notations, signed by the testatrix, declared the will to be null and void. *Id*.

Once you have given the rule and explained the rule fully, the next step is to apply the rule to the client's facts. Your discussion will be a thorough analysis of applicable law as stated in your rule section. Analogize your facts to precedent cases. Distinguish your facts from other precedent cases.

Example:

Here, Daisy would argue that the will was properly canceled when Betty wrote "revoked by Betty Rubble on December 24, 1994," directly across the signatures of Betty and her three witnesses. First, Daisy would argue that Betty clearly intended to revoke her will. Daisy would posit that, based upon the court's analysis in *Casten*, Betty's notation written across her signature and those of her witnesses on December 24, 1994, is a "symbol" of that intent. Fred would, however, submit that *Casten* is inapplicable here, since *Casten* is based upon revocation by burning, and this case presents facts regarding revocation by cancellation.

Your conclusion will resemble the brief answer, but it should include more specific facts. It can, and probably will, be more than one sentence. Think of this short section as a recapitulation of the initial conclusion with factual embellishment.

Outlining

Outline your ideas before writing so that your writing flows. Produce a logical structure for your analysis. Organizing your paragraphs beforehand will make writing easier. Decipher whether your analysis includes a SERIES of elements or a SINGLE element. Are there sub-elements? If so, what is the best order in which to discuss them? It may not necessarily be in the order that the cases discuss them. Move from general rules to more specific rules and exceptions. Use the key legal terms and language discussed in the statute(s) and/or case(s).

Start with the law. What does the statute/leading case say that governs the issue? For example, if your issue concerns a burglary, start by mentioning all the elements of burglary generally. Then focus on those elements that are significant to the legal question in your facts. This should lead to your analysis. Next, see how the cases have addressed the issue. Discuss how each side might analyze the cases (as you did when analogizing and distinguishing). If a case is favorable to the potential client, how would she argue the case? If the same case is not favorable to her, what would she argue? What would her opponent argue about the same case?

Consider how to divide paragraphs most effectively for the reader. Use transitions to help the reader connect one paragraph to another, while signaling a change in focus. For example:

- "The first prong of the *Shubert* analysis requires an assessment of ..."
- "After determining that a compensable injury occurred, the court will next consider ..."
- "The court in *Smith*, unlike that in *Blue*, held that ..."

Your conclusion is a prediction of what you think will happen. You should summarize the result; it should not be more than one solid paragraph.

Do not forget citations. Citation is a way to give credit for thoughts that are not your own. You need a citation for every legal rule or principle you write. You MUST cite a source for any thought you take from a case, **not just a direct quotation**. (See Chapter on Citations.)

Keys to a Great Objective Memo

1. Get a draft done early. Everyone is a better editor than a writer.
2. Revise, revise, revise!
3. Have others read your memo for clarity, flow, typos, etc.
4. Read the memo OUT LOUD to yourself.
5. Punctuation, grammar, spelling, etc., must be PERFECT.

Memorandum Checklist:

A. Have you concentrated on solving a problem rather than writing an essay?
B. Have you edited out waffling?
C. Have you told the reader whether the prediction is qualified in any way?
D. Have you accounted for gaps in the law?
E. Have you accounted for gaps in the facts?

F. Have you refused to hide from bad news?

G. Have you ignored red herrings?

CHAPTER 9

✟

LEGAL PERSUASION AND THE PERSUASIVE MEMORANDUM

The steps and format of the persuasive memorandum is very similar to that of the objective memorandum. However, a good persuasive memorandum is short and direct. There are many persuasive techniques you can employ to write a better product. First, remember what an argument is and what it is for. An argument should be organized to convince the reader to adopt a specific viewpoint. Second, acknowledge your audience. Recognize the appropriate language you may need to use, depending on your audience. Third, construct an influential concept and brainstorm reasons why one would adopt your stance. Trim down your reasons to those that are manageable.

When you have finalized your reasonable arguments, organize them into a logical order. Research legal authority and apply the authority to your concept. Be very explicit in explaining how a particular rule governs your facts. Use particular and precise language to communicate your idea in the best way possible. Acknowledge opposing viewpoints and discuss the strengths and weaknesses of all arguments. Let your words flow logically into your conclusion to make it easier for the reader to agree with your position.

Constructing an argument in this way will lead to a well-organized and decisive conclusion. In persuasive brief writing, employ the same tactics for establishing an argument as set out above.

Format your brief to keep it organized in a cogent manner:

a.   Questions Presented
b.   Introduction
c.   Statement of Case
d.   Statement of Facts
e.   Argument
f.   Conclusion

In persuasive writing, you must make sure you: (1) identify the problem to be addressed; (2) present the legal rule(s) that govern the problem; (3) analyze the rule(s); (4) apply the rule(s) to the specific facts of the problem; and (5) formulate a conclusion that tells the court how the law should resolve the problem.

Remember that the court wants to know your client's view as to the proper legal resolution of the dispute that is in litigation. Assert that view with conviction and offer a favorable solution. Be sure to make a specific request of the court.

Do not forget that you may not misrepresent facts or law to the court. You have a duty to zealously advocate for your client, but you are also an officer of the court. You must face unfavorable facts and law, but do not dwell on them. In arguing, claim that the facts and/or the authorities are not actually unfavorable by using them affirmatively in support of your position. It is not unusual for facts and authorities to be good for one party from one standpoint, but also good for the other party from a different standpoint.

Assert that the facts and the authorities are not relevant to your argument. The case may be decided on another basis. Distinguish facts and authorities. Contend that the facts and law are simply incorrect. Use the following language:

"The court may disregard this fact because it is not material to the application of the rule in this case."

"The court may disregard this case because it does not reflect the law in this jurisdiction on this issue."

"This fact is only unfavorable when combined with certain other facts that are not present in the instant case."

"This case only reached (an unfavorable result) because the court based its decision on a combination of factors that are not all present in the instant case."

"This case assumed the existence of fact x, and that fact is simply not true."

"The court adopted the view of only two other courts, while ten courts have rejected that view."

Order your arguments according to: (1) the strength of the law; and (2) the strength of the equities. If one or two points of your argument are significantly stronger on the law than the others (and this will usually be the case), you should order them by strength, placing the strongest point first. A reader's attention to the argument is greatest at the beginning and drops off rapidly after the first few pages. Judges are busy and want to see the strongest arguments first. A judge will become frustrated with the writer and the writer's client's position if the judge finds that the first arguments are the weaker arguments. Judges tend to presume that the strongest argument is first and thus prejudge the subsequent arguments as even weaker.

Equity speaks to the fair-mindedness of an argument. The court can be persuaded by arguments that something just is not fair. These contentions appeal to the reader's sense of justice and mercy. If your points are of relatively equal legal strength, you may choose to order them according to their factual strength. You will be able to identify which is which by asking yourself, "Which of these points really sounds like an appeal to justice or mercy? Which convinces me that one or more of these parties should win, as opposed to which party is legally supposed to win?" If you have a point that relies heavily on the equities, you should capitalize on these favorable equities directly after discussing the legal arguments. A reader convinced of the justice of your case will be more willing to accept your legal analysis.

Prioritize your issues based on legal rulings rather than equity. For instance, courts normally decide issues in the following order: (1) jurisdictional grounds; (2) procedural grounds; and (3) substantive grounds. Judges often prefer to decide issues on narrow grounds rather than on broad grounds. When both a constitutional ground and a non-constitutional ground are dispositive, constitutional jurisprudence requires courts to decide as many of the issues as possible on the non-constitutional ground.

In rebutting the opposing party's contentions, follow these guidelines:

a. Include counterarguments in your pleading when (1) you are relatively certain that the opposing party or the court will raise the argument; and (2) you can weaken it with a preemptive discussion.

b. Usually, the most effective forms of counterargument do not draw attention to the opposing argument by labeling it as such, e.g., "the defendant may argue that——; however, ——." Instead, articulate YOUR position on a point in more detail than you use to articulate the opposing party's argument. Detail is a technique for emphasis, and lack of detail is a technique for de-emphasis.

c. Do not place an identified counterargument ahead of your own affirmative argument. Rather, place it after you have made all of your own points. Otherwise, your pleading will take on a defensive tone and will lose much of its rhetorical power.

d. After you have a draft of the argument, compare the space devoted to the counterargument with the space devoted to the affirmative argument. The majority of the discussion should be devoted to your own affirmative argument.

e. Avoid emotion, and do not exaggerate or overstate the law or the facts.

Ironically, modifiers that are intended to reinforce a proposition sometimes take away from the strength of an otherwise powerful statement. For example, comments such as "It is abundantly clear" have little effect on the reader, except to make the reader wonder if the words were added to shore up a shaky proposition that is, in fact, subject to debate. The reader may be offended or put off by the fact that the writer feels a need to tell the reader that something is obvious. If the point is obvious, it goes without saying that the reader will know without being told. Most judges will accept your conclusions more readily if you offer persuasive arguments than if you invoke stock phrases that describe your arguments as persuasive.

Keys:

1. Remember your audience: the trial judge, who must apply mandatory authority.
2. Remember the purpose of the memo: to educate and persuade.
3. End with a brief conclusion reminding the court of the relief you seek.

CHAPTER 10

✦

ETHICAL CONSIDERATIONS

A ll attorneys will have a file cabinet full of papers and/or an inbox full of e-mails. We must communicate with our clients, the opposing parties, witnesses, judges, and various other entities in order to assist our clients. This need to communicate and document everything in a written format is quite universal among the various practice areas.

When communicating with a client, the attorneys and their office staff are under certain ethical obligations. Most can be gleaned from good old-fashioned common sense. Don't lie to your client. Don't create false expectations. While these rules and concepts seem so basic, in reality, they are quite complicated.

Imagine a client who is facing a challenging custody battle. She sends you e-mails every other day wanting an update on her case. Her case is set for a hearing in three months. You have other trials next week that need your attention. Can you tell the client to just leave you alone and wait her turn? Can you stop reading or responding to the e-mails? More tempting, can you tell her you have all of her trial work done already when you really don't? After all, what is the harm when you really will have her trial work done well before the hearing?

Imagine you are a personal injury attorney and your client was hit from behind by a tractor-trailer. There is no way your client was at fault. The other driver even admitted he was texting while driving. This will be a really big settlement for your firm. The client e-mails you and is nervous about his case. He wants you to guarantee him that you will win his case or he is going to hire another firm. You assure him that he has a very strong case. He still demands a guarantee. Do you go ahead and tell him you are 100 percent sure he is going to win, or do you try to explain the ethics rules that say you can't guarantee any results?

In today's times, the clients will e-mail, call and/or text you about their cases. Do you breach a line of professionalism when you text your client "IDK" or "LOL?" Or is it better to be a regular, accessible person to your client? Where is the line? Can the client become your friend? Do you bill the client who e-mails you a joke?

The primary considerations in all client communications are honesty and clarity. Tell your clients the truth and make sure they understand it. When the opinion is not good, state it anyway. You do your clients a disservice by beating around the bush and putting a ribbon and a bow on bad news. If you want to be the attorney who is also your client's friend, then you must be that friend who can administer tough love. You cannot let your client think she has a strong case when your research has revealed that she has a weak case. Tell your client the honest results of your diligent research. This can be done in such a manner that the client understands that you are still on her side, but the law is not.

PRACTICAL CONSIDERATIONS

You must read the document while considering the audience. While your clients may be of average or above-average intelligence, you cannot expect them to know the legal jargon that you use on a regular basis. After a few months of law school, law students suddenly begin to talk differently and use words they never used before. This is a normal part of the indoctrination of attorneys. Attorneys speak their own language. This is not unlike how doctors or teachers or mechanics or the employees at Kinko's speak their own language. The problem is that the clients will not understand. Even more dangerously, the clients will think they understand, but actually do not.

Contrary to the images one may see on television, attorneys strive for clarity. It is a sign of poor legal writing when the reader has to scratch his head and read a document again to get a full understanding of the document's contents. If you are writing a letter or a memo to a client or other lay person, the language must be appropriate for your audience. If you can remember back to a time prior to your first semester of law school, you will be in the mindset of your clients. You didn't know what *res judicata* meant, and neither will your client. Unless there is a reason to write differently, always write to an audience who is reasonably intelligent, but does not understand the law.

There are also terms of art that have significance to those in the legal field, but will need further explanation to your client. What is joint custody? Does that mean the dad has the child for six months, and the mom has the child the other six months? While the parents understand the words "joint" and "custody," it is unlikely they will be able to appreciate the legal significance without some guidance from their attorneys. It is extremely important to be able to notice when regular words have special significance and be able to make clear to your clients why you are explaining these words to them. The desire to develop a relationship with your clients will be made more difficult if they think you are talking down to them. Tell the clients why you are explaining what "mandatory authority" versus "persuasive authority" means. While they know what the words mean in general, they have different significance in a legal context.

Suppose you have clients who are not legally sophisticated or have limited reading comprehension. These clients have the ability to assist in their own representation, but may not be able to understand a written letter. Do you not write them and have no written documentation of what you said, or do you write them knowing that they won't understand the letter? Each choice is less than desirable. The answer lies somewhere in between. If the client is illiterate and there is no one who can read the document to the client, it is unnecessary to send a letter. You may need to put a letter in your own file though.

ATTORNEY-CLIENT PRIVILEGE

As a general rule, all communication with your client is privileged and does not have to be revealed to the other parties to the suit. This means that the clients can tell you their concerns without fear you will have to, or be allowed to, share those thoughts/discussions with anyone else. The policy is to allow free-flowing communication between the attorneys and the clients. After all, before the clients signed a retainer agreement, the attorneys were nothing more than strangers. After the contract for legal services is signed, the clients are expected to share the most intimate details of their lives with the stranger, their attorney. Clients know that this rule prohibits an attorney from divulging any personal information shared with that attorney, even if they never finish paying the attorney's retainer fee.

This rule allows the clients to know that even if they never finish paying the attorney the retainer, that attorney cannot use the information against them. The attorney for the plaintiff can't get a bigger fee from the defendant and then decide to represent the defendant and use the plaintiff's information against him.

There is debate as to which forms of communication warrant protection under this privilege. Most attorneys could not function without their e-mail accounts. The courthouse is full of smart phones, and an occasional Blackberry and Netbook. There are unsecured wireless networks everywhere where attorneys take a moment to e-mail their clients about their cases. Do we have a reasonable expectation of privacy when e-mailing a client in general? Does that expectation change when we are on an unsecured wireless network? Some argue that the rules for privilege adapt to the technology. Others say that when you put information into cyberspace, you cannot reasonably expect that it is secure; thus, there is no attorney-client privilege when information is contained in an e-mail. Others distinguish between the methods the parties use to e-mail. They would argue there is an expectation of privacy in an e-mail that is sent from your office network. However, if you are relying on a wireless network, you had notice that the information could be intercepted. Are the rules the same if you are a state employee, a public defender, and the e-mail system is used by the state? The public defender and the district attorney both work for the state. Can they access each other's e-mail accounts? Is it appropriate for them to send e-mails realizing that the other party may have access to the same e-mail database?

The debate on the existence of the privilege also includes the use of cell phones and cordless phones. Can you really have an expectation of privacy when talking on a cell phone? The argument is the same as with e-mails. Some attorneys are using land line phones and insist that their clients do the same. At the same time, a great majority of clients will not likely have a land line to use. Doesn't the law keep up with the technology?

The attorney-client privilege is not absolute. It is the attorney's responsibility to educate the client so the client does not inadvertently cancel the privilege. Firm policies should be in place to routinely advise the clients that a seemingly innocent act may nullify the attorney-client privilege. If the clients nullify the privilege and you have not advised them on how not to do that, you may be responsible for the ramifications.

One common issue is the supportive friend at the attorney-client meeting. The client is going through a tough divorce and brings her friend to the attorney's office for moral support. Another client is disabled and you are fighting to get her disability benefits. Her friend drives her to the attorney's office because she can't drive. Another client is accused of a crime. He did not do it, and he brings his alibi witness with him to your office. These are very reasonable and practical things for the clients to do. However, the presence of third parties during the clients' meeting with their attorney nullifies the privilege to the extent the third party hears the discussion. That third party could be called to testify by the opposing party regarding what he or she heard in your office. Try telling that friend to wait outside for an hour while you talk to your client. Better yet, try explaining to your client that her best friend of 25 years cannot remain in the room because she may decide to share what she has heard. These will not be pleasant conversations. The best case scenario is to avoid the situation by telling the client the rule at the outset of your representation. The rule will be abstract and, thus, the client won't believe that you are attacking her best friend. After all, it is actually rude to tell her friend to wait outside while you talk to your client for an hour. It is rude, but very necessary. There is no way a prudent attorney will take the chance that the client's friend will learn of your trial strategy and be susceptible to being called by the opposing party.

When the client insists that her friend stay in the meeting, you have an obligation to explain the implications; but note that the client owns the privilege and can waive it, against your strong and documented advice. As long as the client understands that her friend can become her enemy and the information you discuss can land in the opposing party's hands, you just go on with your consultation. Note, however, in your file that you suggested that you and the client have a private meeting, but your client refused.

Another common issue is the sharing client. When you send the client a scathing e-mail telling her how awful the other party is, she will gladly forward that e-mail to the other party or a friend. She wants to say, "even my attorney thinks you are a jerk." The problem is that once she shares your communication with another party, the attorney-client privilege is waived as to that communication. Even in court, the sharing client will answer a question and say that she did or did not do something because her attorney advised her. "I stopped responding to his angry e-mails to me because my attorney told me that I did not have to respond after I had already addressed the matter. My attorney said I would not be in contempt of the court order," the sharing client blurts out on the witness stand.

The key is to systematically address these sharing client issues at the outset of your representation. Explain to the clients the implications of sharing your e-mails and telling others what you discussed. Document this discussion in the clients' file and give reminders, as needed.

The clients also need to understand the circumstances where the privilege simply doesn't apply. This brings up the issue of the confessing client. This client decides that you are his confidant, and he wants to tell you exactly what he did. However, in court, he still plans to say he did not do it. This needs to be explained very quickly, especially in a criminal case. Unfortunately, due to unrealistic television shows and bad lawyer jokes, some clients think that attorneys will actively engage in a misrepresentation before the court. Attorneys will not assist you in defrauding the court. If the client sends an e-mail to his attorney alluding to the fact that the client will lie or otherwise deceive the court, the attorney cannot share that e-mail. The attorney has dueling obligations. He cannot share the information, but he also cannot allow the client to deceive the court. Thus, he must withdraw as counsel. To avoid the judge lambasting him for withdrawing in the middle of the case, the common buzz words are "the rules of professional responsibility require that I withdraw." Hopefully, this will subtly inform the judge that you have a good reason for withdrawing; it is so good, you can't even tell him.

The confessing client should have been advised that if he confesses to you one version of the events, you cannot be his attorney if he wants to go to court and tell the court another version of the events. Thus, you must tell the client the limitations on your ability to represent him. Tell him you have an obligation to be truthful before the court. Despite what television show he watched, tell him you will not create a document or state anything to the court that is untrue. He must then decide what to tell you. Hopefully, there is only one version of events, but it is the client's prerogative to decide what he does and does not want to share.

Lastly, the client needs to know that your obligation to the safety of others supersedes the attorney-client privilege. Though not all threats nullify the privilege, if the client makes a viable threat against someone, the attorney has an obligation to act for the safety of the other party, even if that compromises the attorney-client privilege. If the client tells you that he is "going to go kill his ex-wife," you have an obligation to do something about it. You still must use good judgment in dealing with the situation. Contact the police or engage in a reasonable effort to prevent your client from doing bodily harm. You need only break the privilege to the extent necessary to prevent the immediate harm. Even if the threat warranted a nullification of the privilege, this does not open the door to allow the attorney to share other information unrelated to the threat. For example, if the client threatened to kill the ex-wife, the attorney may act for the safety of the ex-wife if the threat was viable, but the attorney cannot share the information that the client confessed regarding how he killed his last girlfriend.

The ethical obligations you have to society as a whole complicates the attorney-client relationship. At the outset of your representation, tell the client what information you have that obliges you to share it with others. Don't let the client put you in a situation where you have to discern the viability of a threat. You should not be the person the client contacts when he is just venting. A prudent attorney would likely err on the side of protecting the third party and share the information, to the chagrin of the client who was likely just having a bad day and venting. Avoid this situation by letting the client know the limitations of the privilege.

CHAPTER 11

☥

CORRESPONDENCE

ENGAGEMENT LETTERS

After the client has retained your firm's services, it is common to write an engagement letter that reiterates key points from your initial consultation and summarizes the role of your firm in the matter. The letter details that you have said all of those little things you intended to say to all of your clients, i.e., the scope of attorney-client privilege, the scope of representation, etc. Most importantly, the letter establishes the tone for your representation. Generally, the letter should be around two or three pages.

Greeting/Introduction. In this section, you should introduce yourself to the client in case you have not already met or talked on the phone. Tell the client your role in the firm. Are you an associate attorney? Have you been assigned as the primary contact in the case? Be gracious and thank the client for choosing your law firm. Tell the client why you are writing this letter to him. The purpose is likely to review the facts, explain the firm's plan of action, and open the doors of communication.

Facts. In this section, you will briefly recap the facts the client gave you or a member of the firm. Particularly, if you were not present at the initial meeting, it is important for the client to know that you have a command of the facts. State the facts truthfully, yet with sensitivity. You cannot amend the facts to spare your client's feelings. If she did something wrong or embarrassing, she needs to get comfortable discussing it with you. "You acknowledge that you had been drinking at least two beers before you drove the car that night. However, it is unclear whether you had exceeded the legal limit." If there are emotional facts, only state them if they are truly necessary to the case. For example, if the client has a deadly disease, you do not need to mention that if the case is a bankruptcy case designed to prevent a foreclosure. The cancer will not be relevant. However, if you are trying to show compassion, then you can discuss the purely emotional fact briefly in the introduction section. "I regret that you have cancer. I know you are dealing with quite a bit, physically. I will do my best to ensure that the bankruptcy proceeding is as time efficient as possible, limiting your need to come to court as much as feasible. The purpose of this letter is to …" You should have some gauge on the client and decide if the client would rather not discuss the nonlegal matter at all with you. If the client has cancer, but it is clear that the client would not like to discuss the cancer, then there is no need to mention it.

Address the client and parties appropriately. "You and Mr. Dunk were riding in the back seat at the time of the accident." It is highly recommended that you address the clients by their last names. If the clients insist on being called by their first names, feel free to do so. The idea is simply to establish a tone of professionalism. You may refer to the opposing parties by their last names or by their role in the case. You may say "Defendant" or "Mr. Tamil." When children are involved, it is recommended that you refer to them by their first names. Calling the child, "the minor child" or by his surname may cause you to appear cold and disinterested, or too rigid and formal.

Scope of Representation. Be very clear about what you and the firm are doing for the client. If you are going to trial, explain what will happen if the case needs to go to the appellate courts on appeal. Will your firm file the appeal? Will you need to execute a new fee agreement? Be sure the clients understand that any decisions you make in their case are still governed by the rules of ethics. For example, you may agree to file the appeal, but if you determine that there are no appealable issues, you cannot file the appeal in good faith. So you tell the client, "If legally warranted, our firm will file an appeal for you to the N.C. Court of Appeals."

It is common to have a limited scope of representation. Your firm is free to limit the representation as you deem appropriate. The retainer is a private contract, and the parties can negotiate and agree on the terms contained therein. There are broad sweeping rules regarding outrageous fees, etc. The State Bar prohibits attorneys from charging large amounts and doing very little to no work. However, generally, the parties have the freedom to contract. You can agree to only do research, write a brief, go to trial or participate in mediation. The most important point is that the scope of the representation must be clear to the clients.

Explanation of the Law. In this section, you are giving the client a basic understanding of the law. You are to demonstrate to the client that you possess competence regarding the general area of the law and then discuss the special circumstances of the client's matter. If further research will be needed, tell the client. It is perfectly acceptable to let the client know that you have been presented with a fairly novel situation, and you need to find the case precedent or legal authority that addresses the issue specifically. The clients will understand and appreciate the fact that you are not treating their case with a cookie-cutter approach. After all, most clients do believe their case is different than any other case you have had, and they are often correct.

Remember that the attorneys' role is to explain and not merely cite the law. Avoid too many quotations of the law in communications to the client. If the clients could readily understand the case without the attorneys' help, there would be no reason to write the explanatory letters to the clients. The clients rely on and expect their attorneys to take the complex legal rules and make them simple and understandable. If the case or statute is very clear, this would be the rare time when you should quote the law for the client. If you do quote, be very careful to redact anything that is not relevant. While this is a good practice in general, it is even more important when communicating with a client. The clients will not be able to decipher or discern the relevant portion from the irrelevant portion and will assume all of the law you are referencing applies to their case. Do not give the clients this extraneous information. If the statute has twelve factors, only mention the factors relating directly to your client's case.

Avoid unnecessary details in your explanation of the law. The clients generally want you to deal specifically with their case. They generally do not appreciate or understand generic overviews of the law. The clients will not be pleased to learn about the twenty-plus exceptions to the hearsay requirement, only to discover that none of them apply to their case. It is tempting to share your vast knowledge with the clients. Attorneys do believe that the law is truly fascinating. The clients will agree, as long as the law we are fascinated with directly impacts their lives. We must be respectful of our clients' time as well. Save the exciting discussions about the law for the office parties.

While quotations to the law should be held to a minimum, it is quite appropriate to cite authority. Some argue that the clients will not need to know the names of the cases or the statutes. However, many clients are very interested in knowing the law. They want to engage in a real discussion with you and not just have you tell them your opinion. They have access to the Internet and different advocacy websites and may be able to pull the cases or statutes and read them.

When you are citing, you can take some liberty with traditional Bluebook rules. In general, you should cite the cases, as required by the rules. However, when there is a particular Bluebook rule that would cause the client to misunderstand or get confused about what you are saying, you can adjust your usage of the standard rules. For example, after the long cite of a case, if there are no intervening cites, you must use *Id.* to cite the short cite of the case. In a letter to a client, you may opt to state the case name again, instead of using *Id.* Example: In *State v. Mullins*, the defendant was acquitted because the felon rule had not been adopted by the state legislature. *State v. Mullins*, 112 N.C. 57 (1999). However, the court held that it was in error to dismiss the attempted murder charge. *Mullins*.

In the example above, the Bluebook rules would have required *Id.* to be used for the short cite. However, most clients would probably not understand what *Id.* means. The threshold standard is to give proper attribution to the authority you are using. It is inappropriate to fail to cite authority, even in client correspondences.

Steps in the Proceeding. Here, you must take the time to discuss the overall legal process. These steps should be specific to your clients' case. If this is a civil matter, you can explain the basic things that can be expected, such as the discovery process, depositions, etc. The clients should gain a greater appreciation for what you will be doing on their case as well. For example, if you are going to file a lengthy brief next week, the clients should know that is a part of the process. If you are sending the client a detailed opinion letter in three weeks, you should say so. Helping the clients understand what is going on is critical to having happy clients. Attorneys are often working very hard on their clients' cases, but then get frustrated when the angry clients call to complain because presumably nothing is going on in their case. The problem is that the attorneys never communicated to the clients what they were doing.

Explaining the steps can help shape the clients' understanding of the time that it will take to get the matters resolved. Television shows have really ruined the perception of our profession. On television, we appear fascinating and always in court arguing for immediate relief, and all situations are resolved in an hour. The reality is that most legal matters take months and years to resolve, not hours and days. If you are going to file a complaint, the client should know that there is a 30-day (and often a 60-day) period before the next notable action takes place. If you tell the clients that there will be 60 days before you get the response to the complaint, the clients will understand that they do not need to follow up in a week.

Take your time and explain the steps carefully. The clients rarely know what to expect in a case. Let the engagement letter serve as their guide. If done properly, this document will alleviate lots of anxiety. The clients can refer back to this section of the document and remind themselves where their case is in the process.

Mediation. Most clients only think of going to court to fight about the outcome that they want. The various forms of alternative dispute resolution are becoming more and more accepted in the legal justice system. In fact, many courts require mediation. All courts encourage it. If you must engage in court-ordered mediation, tell the clients what that process means. Will the attorney be able to attend the mediation? Will the parties be in the same room? Different courts have different rules, and your clients should know the logistics of the mediation so they can be mentally prepared to attend. If an angry husband must sit in the same room as the wife who left him, he may need to prepare himself for this encounter. If the shy, non-confrontational client has to attend the mediation without his attorney, he may need to be advised of that as well.

Explain the mediation options. If there are options regarding whether to attend mediation, who the mediator should be, or the terms and the scope of the mediation, tell the client about the choices. While the attorneys' input is critical here, these are ultimately the client's decisions. Some courts let the parties choose between a private mediation session with the attorneys present or a session without the attorney. The differences are great, so the decision is important. There are considerations regarding the costs. The private mediator costs more than the court-appointed mediator. However, most attorneys think the mediations are more productive when the attorneys are present. This preference exists not merely because attorneys place a high value on their services, but in reality, the attorneys have researched the strengths and weaknesses of the clients' cases and know where there are places that bargaining would be essential.

Explain the rules of confidentiality. As a general rule, the information gleaned during mediation cannot be used at trial against the party. Further, the settlement proposals that are discussed in mediation cannot be used against a party at trial. For example, Defendant can get on the stand at trial and state that he does not ever plan to pay the plaintiff anything. The plaintiff cannot cross examine the Defendant and introduce evidence that the defendant offered the plaintiff a settlement during mediation. These rules are designed to encourage open and frank settlement discussions. Being openly candid with the opposing party is something that the client is likely uncomfortable with, and knowing these rules may offer some comfort to the client.

Explain the mediation strategy. You and the clients need to agree on the positions you will take and the information you can divulge in the mediation. The results of your research should greatly influence and define your mediation strategy. At the point you are writing the engagement letter, you would not have engaged in enough research to have a complete mediation strategy. It will be sufficient to let the clients know that you are thinking about the strategy, researching it, and will be ready to discuss it in a few weeks (or days).

It is imperative for the attorney and the clients to be in agreement on the terms that can be agreed upon in mediation. Ultimately, it is the clients' decision to decide whether to settle the case. The attorney has an ethical obligation to only communicate the position that the clients have authorized her to communicate. Letting the clients know that they control the process, with your guidance, may offer them assurance.

Explain the effects of the results. If an agreement is reached in mediation, the agreement will be signed by a judge and will be an enforceable court order. The clients may not realize that they are executing a document that will become a court order since they are not in court and there is no judge present. It is the attorneys' obligation to ensure the clients understand what they are signing. If they sign the agreement in mediation, they will not "get their day in court." However, they will get the effect of the court order.

Court. Here, you can discuss logistics of the court hearing, if there is a hearing. You can explain what to expect in the trial preparation process. How would you prepare the clients and their witnesses for the hearing? You can briefly discuss courtroom etiquette, as you deem appropriate. Some clients will need more guidance in this area than others. You do not help your clients when you don't inform them of things that they should know, and the strength of their case is often compromised. Be careful not to offend your clients by telling them that this is general advice that you tell all of your clients.

Items I need From You. This is the section that gives the clients a clear list of the items you need from them. Often, the clients may arrive in your office after they have been served with a complaint. You will need to file the response to a pleading or discovery. Don't simply give the clients the discovery and ask them to get you the items. Create the list for them in a manner that is easy to understand. If the discovery has a request for items that you do not intend to produce, tell the clients. You may want to see the items, but advise the clients that you are going to go through them and ensure you are answering the questions appropriately. For example, if the discovery request asks for materials that are attorney-client privileged or would be unduly burdensome to produce, let the clients know that you may want them to attempt to collect the documents so you can review them, but you will not likely produce them to the other side for their review if they are in fact outside the scope of discovery or privileged. However, you cannot make the determination regarding the discoverability of the documents without reviewing them. The clients also must understand the time frames that you and the court have. You will need to get the documents to the opposing party in a certain number of days. The clients need to get you the documents in enough time for you to review them before you have to produce them to the other party.

Attorney's Fees. Your firm would have already executed a written contract with the client. However, it would be appropriate to reiterate the basic terms of the agreement. Make sure the clients understand the costs of their services, particularly how your firm tracks its billable hours.

Conclusion. At the end of the letter, it would be necessary to clarify any contact protocols or other matters that you like to address with your clients. For example, if you generally contact clients weekly by e-mail, you should let them know that. Regular communication is extremely important, but only communicate with the clients when it is necessary. If you send the clients an e-mail on Friday afternoon when nothing is going on with their case, they will not be as appreciative of the communication when they get the monthly bill.

OPINION LETTERS

After you have done your research on the clients' issues, it is time to share these findings and recommendations with the clients. You should know that the clients are anticipating this letter. You would have told them when the letter was coming and, undoubtedly, they marked their calendars. Within the opinion letter, you explain the firm's legal position on the clients' legal matters. You will discuss the relevant precedent cases in great detail. You will walk the clients through how you have compared and contrasted the precedent cases with the clients' current situation.

Introduction. Clearly state the firm's legal opinion. Be careful not to overstate your opinion or guarantee results.

Example:

Inappropriate: You will win on all issues.

Appropriate: Based on our research, you have a strong likelihood of success on the issues.

Your recommendations should be unambiguous, while still acknowledging that these are not dictates to the clients.

Example:

Inappropriate: You must file a voluntary dismissal of your counterclaims that you had previously filed *pro se*.

Appropriate: It is our legal opinion that the counterclaims you previously filed *pro se* are without legal merit. We recommend that you voluntarily dismiss them.

Even if there is something you firmly believe the client must do, you still cannot require the client to do it. Your remedy is to withdraw from the case, which is not always an easy thing to do.

Facts. Summarize the facts of the clients' case. If you have previously written a comprehensive engagement letter, you have already demonstrated to the clients that you understand the facts of their case. The opinion letter is where you should briefly recap the pertinent facts that impact the legal analysis and ultimate outcome of the case. Be sure to include any new facts that have developed since you wrote the engagement letter.

Discussion of the law. Your task is to give the clients an accurate and clear explanation of the law that supports your legal opinion and assessment of the case. Use a CRAC format: conclusion, rule, analysis, and conclusion again. Do this for each issue that you will address for the clients.

a. **Conclusion**: Restate the firm's legal opinion. State it more succinctly than you did in the introduction section.

b. **Rule**: This is where you state the synthesized rule. In other words, use a combination of the statutes and rules that you gleaned from the cases to state a basic rule that pulls all of these sources together. If you merely insert a quote from a statute or case, you may have stated a correct rule, but that is not a synthesized rule. Good analysis requires you to synthesize, i.e., pull all of your sources of authority together.

c. **Analysis**: Give the facts, holding, and rationale for the case precedent. Then, in a step-by-step approach, explain the ways the case precedent is similar to and different from the clients' case. Explain the significance of these similarities and differences. Repeat this process for each case you wish to address.

d. **Conclusion**: Briefly restate the firm's position on the issue.

Repeat this CRAC format for each issue that you need to address. When in doubt about whether to separate two issues, go ahead and discuss them separately. This will generally help the clients better understand the matters that are being addressed.

Conclusion. Summarize the firm's legal position and state how this position will impact the case. Invite the clients to come in to the office to discuss the strategy after they have read the opinion letter. Welcome the clients' input. Be prepared for the clients who do not take bad news well. Remember, unless you were a judge on the court when the precedent cases were decided, or unless you were a legislator who voted for the statute, you do not have to defend the law. You are merely explaining the law. Often, you will not agree with the case precedent. Tell the clients that they can certainly disagree. They can even bring appeals to challenge what they feel are erroneous court rulings. However, none of us has the luxury of merely ignoring the precedent cases. We may argue stringently that the precedent cases are different from our case; however, we must follow mandatory authority.

General Considerations.

1. Use an eye-friendly font style and size. Feel free to use fonts larger than you would use in a court document. If your clients wear glasses or are otherwise visually impaired, ask them if they have a preference as to font style or size.

2. Page limits. While there are no page limits, it is important to use appropriate judgment when communicating with the clients. Engagement letters are usually two–three pages long. Opinion letters are usually less than 10 pages.

3. Double-space the text of the documents, except quotes that are 50 words or more.

4. Avoid the legal jargon (legalese). There are so many phrases that have no significance to the non-attorney. Your goal is to explain the law to the client in a way that the client can understand it.

COVER LETTERS

Write a strong letter to the other attorneys that outlines your proposal. Give the attorneys a preview of your research. It is important to show the opposing party that you are aware of the strengths of your case and that you have researched the matter. At the same time, you do not want to do the other party's research for them. State your position and tell the opposing party about a positive case in your favor. There is, however, no need to fully explain the case to the opposing side.

SETTLEMENT PROPOSALS

The key to writing a strong settlement proposal is to be as accurate and complete as possible. Settlement proposals can come in various formats. If you are settling a workers' compensation claim, you will need to include exhibits with your proposal. Your exhibits will be documents that address your client's medical condition, bills, etc. If you are settling a custody case or other civil court matter, you will need to write a consent order. With the agreement of all parties, this can be submitted to the judge for signature.

In a comprehensive consent order, all reasonably foreseeable contingencies are addressed. For example, if you are writing a proposed order to resolve a custody case, you should address school schedules and summer schedules. The recipient of your proposal should be able to read the proposal and know exactly where the child will be at any given point in time.

In a comprehensive settlement brochure for a workers' compensation claim, the recipient of the proposal should be clear on your allegations regarding all damages alleged, and any other outstanding issues that impact the resolution of the case.

CHAPTER 12

✝

CITATIONS

WHEN TO CITE

Students often ask if they should have a citation after every sentence. The obvious answer is no. The question comes from a basic fear of committing plagiarism and/or an attempt to not truly figure out the rules regarding when a citation is required. There are times when it is absolutely required that the writer include a citation. The writer must always cite when he is stating the holding of the case and the court's rationale. There can be no debate that the court's holding and rationale were not the product of the writer's individual ideas.

One common error is to simply include a citation at the end of each paragraph. The citation is only able to provide attribution to the preceding sentence, not the entire paragraph.

Example:

In *Jones v. Smith*, the court held that there was no police officer exception to the "no guns in schools" policy that had been adopted by the school board. *Jones v. Smith*, 12 N.C. 13, 14, 345 S.E.2d 456, 457 (2009). This is a case of first impression in North Carolina. However, there is ample authority in other jurisdictions for this policy. This case follows the same line of reasoning as several New York cases. In *New York Concerned Parents, Inc. v. City of New*

York, the plaintiffs were successful in arguing that off-duty police officers could not have their guns on them at school events. *New York Concerned Parents, Inc. v. City of New York*, 345 N.E.2d 234 (2007). Both cases are similar in that each school district had previously adopted a "no guns" policy, and intended to have no exceptions to their policy. *Jones*, 12 N.C. at 16; *New York Concerned Parents, Inc.*, 344 N.E.2d at 236. In *New York Concerned Parents, Inc.*, the parents were concerned about the danger that guns could be accessed by students. *Id.*

In the example, there was not a citation after every sentence. The citations were only needed when the writer was referencing the specific facts and holding in the cases.

Citation Clauses v. Citation Sentences

While it is more common to use citation sentences, citation clauses are appropriate to use as well. A citation clause serves as an interrupting clause in a sentence, and it is set off by commas before and after the citation. In contrast, the citation sentence is at the end of the sentence the citation references. The citation sentence is concluded with a period.

Example:

There is no lawful usage of marijuana in North Carolina, even for a medicinal purpose, with a prescription. *Baker v. North Carolina*, 123 N.C. 456, 789 S.E.2d 101 (2008). However, there have been attempts to carve out narrow exceptions in an effort to overcome a constitutional challenge, *Gates v. Comm'r of Agric.*, 123 S.C. 456 (2009), but these efforts have been met with little success or very restrictive holdings.

The citation to *Baker* goes after the sentence it is referencing. Again, it is a sentence and is concluded with a period. The citation to *Gates*, however, is in the middle of the sentence and is set off by commas.

Basic Citation Rules

As you have realized when you first opened your Bluebook, it contains an assortment of rules. Most of the rules for citation are in the Bluebook. Notably, however, specific local rules for various jurisdictions are not located in the Bluebook. This should cause a feeling of confidence since you can go to one book and find everything you need. Unfortunately, the Bluebook can be overwhelming, intimidating, and frustrating to new users. There are some seeming contradictions in the Bluebook. The basic structure requires use to become acclimated to the rules contained therein. Indeed, there is an internal logic to the Bluebook. There is a systematic method to approach constructing citations.

Step 1. Open the book.

While this may seem a bit too easy to be a legitimate step, it is not. Students are often intimidated by the Bluebook and do not open it. Students have commented that they thought the Bluebook was "the devil." Be assured, it is not. It is a useful tool. The purpose of the Bluebook is to have a uniform set of citations, and to give the author and reader a uniform method of referring to and finding a referenced source. Before the Bluebook, there were common citation forms, but there was no universally accepted resource for those forms. Imagine the utility of being able to go to one book to verify that "Comm." was the common reference for "Committee," not "Community."

By opening the Bluebook, you will immediately see the basic structure. The inside front cover has a quick reference for law review footnotes, and the inside back cover has a quick reference for most of the common primary authority. How can a book with most of the pertinent examples in the inside covers be that bad?

Step 2. Explore the index.

The Bluebook has a very comprehensive index. This is a valuable tool when you are attempting to cite authority for a less orthodox source. For example, you will find exactly how to cite a yearbook by looking up that word in the index. The same rule is true for "United Nations Reports of International Arbitration Awards" and "Radio Broadcasts." While you will not stumble upon the exact citation for every source by simply looking in the index for that source, it is certainly a reasonable and logical place to start.

Step 3. Explore the blue pages.

At the front of the Bluebook, after the Contents and Introduction, there are about 40 blue pages. These pages are an extended quick reference guide for practitioners. There, you will find more examples of the basic citation forms as they pertain to documents commonly filed by practitioners. You will also find a summary of approximately 80 percent of the rules you will use to cite primary and secondary authority. There are also jurisdictionally specific references to certain courts and statutes.

You have access to an extraordinary amount of information before you get into the nuts and bolts of the Bluebook. After reviewing the quick references and the blue pages, you should already have a basic understanding of how citations look. Consider the quick references and blue pages as general rules. The items inside the white pages of the Bluebook are the specific rules, and specific rules always trump the general rules. Thus, if you stumble upon a rule in the white pages that appears to be different than the way you saw the rule in the quick references or the blue pages, follow the rule in the white pages.

Step 4. Check out the various tables.

The tables are the white pages with blue exterior margins located near the back of the Bluebook. Many of your citation questions will deal with how to abbreviate certain words. There are a series of abbreviation tables in the Bluebook. Critics (like the authors of this book) suggest that the abbreviation tables would be easier to follow if there were just one large table. Instead, the Bluebook's abbreviation tables are broken into categories.

Table 1: United States Jurisdictions. Here, you will find information needed to complete all citations to primary authority for federal and state jurisdictions. This is a useful guide when you are trying to determine what the names of the courts are in a specific jurisdiction. The first court that is listed under each jurisdiction (federal or state) is the highest court, and then the other courts are listed in descending order. For example, Table 1 shows that the highest federal court is the United States Supreme Court, while the highest court in North Carolina is the Supreme Court, and the highest court in New York is the Court of Appeals.

Table 2: Foreign Jurisdictions. This table addresses the same material as Table 1, but it only includes information for jurisdictions other than the United States.

Table 3: Intergovernmental Organizations. Here, the Bluebook addresses how you cite to organizations like the United Nations, which have governance powers encompassing multiple countries.

Table 4: Treaty Sources. This table assists in referencing official, unofficial, and intergovernmental treaty sources.

Table 5: Arbitral Reporters. Some arbitration decisions are published, and this table shows how to cite to the arbitration reporters.

Table 6: Case Names. When citing a case name, if a word in that case name appears in this table, you must abbreviate it accordingly. If the word is eight letters or more, you may abbreviate the word if using an abbreviation would save substantial space, and the abbreviation would not create any confusion. As a general rule, do not abbreviate an eight-letter word with a six-letter abbreviated word. Additionally, do not use an abbreviation that could easily be mistaken for another word.

Table 7: Court Names. In addition to the federal and state courts listed in Table 1, there are quite a few specialized courts found in this table. Check first under Table 1 to see if the name of the court is listed there. If the court is not listed there, then check Table 7.

Table 8: Explanatory Phrases. When you want to note prior or subsequent history of a case, you should look here. For example, if an appeal in a case was dismissed or the petition for writ of *certiorari* was denied, this may be essential information that needs to be reflected in the citation. These explanatory phrases may not be required unless they are particularly relevant.

Table 9: Legislative Documents. Here, you will find a list of abbreviations for words that relate to legislative documents. If Table 6 does not contain the information you need, take a quick glance at this table if the citation is to a commonly used legislative document.

Table 10: Geographic Terms. In this table, there are abbreviations for each state in the United States and its territories and practically every country. When citing to an unfamiliar location, you are encouraged to look at this table and not to merely assume that Bluebook abbreviations always mirror the common abbreviations for that location.

Table 11: Judges and Officials. In this table, there are the abbreviations for the titles of judges and various judicial officials. The abbreviation for more than one judge may surprise you.

Table 12: Months. This is where you will find the abbreviations for the months of the year. Months with four letters or less have no abbreviations.

Table 13: Periodicals. Practically every legal periodical that exists is listed in this table. Also use the words listed in this table to craft the citation for periodicals that are specifically listed here. For example, it is clear from the list of abbreviations that "law journal" should be abbreviated "L.J." Thus, while the "Gibson Law Journal" is not listed in this table, it should be cited as the "Gibson L.J." Note there was no space between the "L" and the "J."

Table 14: Publishing Terms. Like Table 8, this table offers additional terms that may be used when referencing a published document. For example, if you are citing a source that is a draft or is a working paper, it would likely be very helpful to the reader to have this information in the citation.

Table 15: Services. Some boutique reporters, guides, and other helpful materials are listed here. If you have a publication that is not found in any of the other tables, take a moment to be sure it has not been listed in Table 15. In essence, this table serves as a bit of a catchall.

Table 16: Subdivisions. Sometimes when you are citing to a very specific part of a source, you will find this table helpful in assisting you to identify the way you cite the part or provision.

Step 6: Check out the Rules section.

The pages of the Rules section are white with blue trim at the top.

To tab or not to tab

Once you have explored the Bluebook, you will now be in a position to organize the rules for yourself. One commonly used method is to insert tabs in different sections of the bluebook. If you are researching in a city jurisdiction, you may find it helpful to tab that jurisdiction's rules in certain tables. This process will help you find frequently cited materials in a more expeditious manner. However, this is completely optional.

SIGNALS

Citing authority without any preceding word to clarify or qualify its connection to the text represents that the citation directly states the proposition, or identifies a quotation or authority with which the citation is associated, e.g. There is a standard set of clarifying or qualifying words (commonly known as introductory signals) used with citations. Placed in front of a citation, these words are italicized (or underlined). When instead these signals form the verb of a sentence that includes a particular citation, they are not italicized (or underlined). No comma separates the signal from the rest of the citation, except for "e.g." which needs a comma before and after it. Only the signal beginning a citation sentence has its initial letter capitalized. The standard signals include:

(a) Signals that indicate support.

E.g.,—Authority states the proposition with which the citation is associated. Other authorities, not cited, do as well. "E.g.," used with other signals (in which case it is preceded by a comma), similarly indicates the existence of other authorities not cited.

Accord—Used following citation to authority referred to in text when there are additional authorities that either state or clearly support the proposition with which the citation is associated, but the text refers to or quotes only one. Similarly, the law of one jurisdiction may be referenced as being in accord with that of another.

See—Used when authority supports the proposition with which the citation is associated either implicitly or in the form of dicta.

See also—Authority is additional support for the proposition with which the citation is associated (but less direct than that indicated by "see" or "accord"). "See also" is commonly used to refer readers to authorities already cited or discussed. The use of a parenthetical explanation of the source material's relevance following a citation introduced by "see also" is encouraged.

Cf.—Authority supports by analogy "Cf." literally means "compare." The citation will only appear relevant to the reader if it is explained. Consequently, parenthetical explanations of the analogy are strongly recommended.

(b) Signals that suggest a useful comparison.

Compare ... with ... —Comparison of authorities that support a particular proposition. Either side of the comparison can have more than one item linked with "and." Parenthetical explanations of comparison are strongly recommended.

(c) Signals that indicate contradiction.

Contra—Authority directly states the contrary of the proposition with which the citation is associated.

But see—Authority clearly supports the contrary of the proposition with which citation is associated.

But cf.—Authority supports the contrary of the position with which the citation is associated by analogy. Parenthetical explanations of the analogy are strongly recommended. The word "but" is omitted from the signal when it follows another negative signal.

(d) Signals that indicate background material.

See generally—Authority presents useful background. Parenthetical explanations of the source materials' relevance are encouraged.

(e) Combining a signal with "e.g."

E.g., in addition to the cited authority, connotes that there are numerous others that state, support, or contradict the proposition (with the other signal indicating which) but citation to them would not be helpful or necessary. The preceding signal is separated from "e.g." by a comma.

CHAPTER 13

✝

EXAM WRITING

There are three steps to success in law school: class preparation, studying, and learning how to play the game (learning to write the essay). While these steps are not necessarily earth-shattering revelations, they are essential, primarily because law students often combine certain steps and skip others.

Class Preparation. In a time crunch, the student has to decide whether to read the case or scan an old outline and rely on the supplements. The answer is always to read the case. A hornbook or supplement will never give you the experience of going through the court's analysis provided in the case. When you have read the case for yourself, there is a heightened understanding, because you have walked through the process with the court. Adequate class preparation allows you to follow the discussion in class much better. Often law professors do not have "canned" lectures in which they stand before the class and explain the cases and the rules of law. In fact, this is very rare in law school. The Socratic Method is a more common teaching tool. Using this method, professors will ask the students provocative questions designed to help the students delve deeper into an analysis of a case or particular issue from a case. The assumption is that the students have read and understood the black-letter law from the cases, and the class discussion is meant to go deeper into policy implications, exceptions to the rules, etc. The student who has not read the cases and not prepared for class will be in no position to engage in an in-depth discussion with his professor or colleagues. Further, the student who expects to sit back in a law school class and gain the basic information by listening to the discussion will be sadly disappointed.

To be in a position to gain additional insight from the professor, students must have at least a basic grasp of the subject matter to be discussed when they enter the class. The professors stand in the classrooms as experts in the chosen subjects. However, the students have to be in a position to engage their professors in vigorous discussion. If the students are struggling to understand the basic concepts, the professors will not be able to have fruitful discussions about the intricacies of the rules, the exceptions, or policy considerations.

When the students keep up with the readings in the syllabus, they have less anxiety and panic when exam time arrives. The students have a basic understanding and exposure to all of the material that was covered during the semester. When they begin to focus on exam preparation, the students will feel more prepared and less overwhelmed. They may need to refresh their memory on a few topics and seek clarity regarding a few others. However, none of the information should be unfamiliar. Lastly, adequate class preparation assists students in identifying if and when they are experiencing problems with the material. Most legal concepts are building blocks to the other concepts. In other words, you must understand the matters that are addressed in Chapter 1 to fully understand what is discussed in Chapter 2 of your casebook. If you never read the cases or understood the concepts of offer and acceptance, then you will be most confused when you begin to hear about the various contract defenses that exist. If you read the materials as they are discussed, you can more easily identify where you need to seek additional support to grasp the concepts. If you have not been consistently prepared for class, you could find yourself trying to master major legal concepts just before the final exam.

Studying. Studying is a separate step from class preparation, because it is distinct and must be treated as such. A common problem in law school is that many students are so concerned about being called on in class, they devote all of their time to reading the cases. When it is time to take the exam, those students think they are adequately prepared for the exam because they spent lots of time reading the cases to be prepared for class. Unfortunately, the students who spend all of their time preparing for class and do not study will be disappointed in their performance on the exams.

Studying requires students to outline their materials. Creating an organized structure in which they can review the cases and their lecture notes is essential to understanding how the body of law students have learned actually comes together. As students are creating their outlines, they are engaging in an important process. They are synthesizing the materials they have read about throughout the course. During this process of pulling the cases together, students should realize where there are matters that require their further exploration or seek additional clarification. At this point, a study group or a meeting with the professor would be helpful. Because the questions are based on their synthesis of the materials, students will have insightful and thoughtful questions.

After they have finished outlining, students must study the outlines and engage in an appropriate amount of discussion with students who have engaged in an equal amount of private studying. Studying the outline causes students to become familiar with the rules of law. Preparation for a law school examination requires students to know certain rules, based on memory. The more important skill is the ability to apply these rules to a given set of facts. However, students must know the rules of law to have any chance of applying them effectively. They must review the outlines and know the black-letter law. Reading cases is not the best way to acquire this skill. A review of the students' own outlines is the most effective way to become familiar with the synthesized rules of law.

Learning how to play the game. This is the last step, and it separates those who merely know the law from those who know the law and perform well in law school. At this point, the students have read all of the cases, written their own outlines and studied them. To demonstrate that knowledge on a law school exam, it takes a bit of additional research. This is research about your professor. If you know that Professor Beckwith tests from the materials you discussed in class, while Professor Ringer prefers to test the rules with more than two steps in the analysis and Professor Amana tests the exceptions to the rules, you might be in a better position to prepare for the test. Does Professor Fox prefer that you write using the IRAC format, while Professor Morris prefer that you write using the CRAC method? This knowledge will be helpful after you have diligently prepared for class and studies, as mentioned above.

Many law professors will share their old exams and perhaps their old grade sheets with you. If these resources are available, you should use them. You should also complete the old exams under timed conditions in a testing environment. Read the fact pattern and prepare an answer. If your professor will read or discuss the answer with you, take advantage of that. Insights from the professor regarding how he/she grades exams will be priceless.

Even if you do not have guidance from the professors as to their preferences, consider the following suggestions as general guidelines.

1. Use IRAC or CRAC. These are familiar formats to all law professors. These formats help you to start out strong in your answers. At the outset, let the professors know that they are about to read a good answer. Show them you know the issues that are being raised based on the facts, and that you know the likely conclusion.
2. Plan before you write.
3. Write.
4. Proofread. While there is limited time during the exams, you need to save a few moments to proofread and correct any obvious errors. Even though you may have felt rushed to write the answer, the professors will probably not make many allowances for grammatical errors, typographical errors, etc. After all, when they are grading your essay, they cannot tell whether you overlooked something or you simply did not know the grammar rule. Thus, errors are all treated as errors on the law school exam. While there will be more points deducted for substantive areas, the grammatical and typographical errors will also result in point deductions.

APPENDICES

APPENDIX A

✝

OUTLINING RULES

A lawyer's fee shall be reasonable. The factors to be considered in determining the reasonableness of a fee include the following: the time and labor required; the novelty and difficulty of the question involved, and the skill requisite to perform the legal service properly; the likelihood, if apparent to the client, that the acceptance of the particular employment will preclude other employment by the lawyer; the fee customarily charged in the locality for similar legal services; the amount involved and the results obtained; the time limitations imposed by the client; the experience, reputation, and ability of the lawyers performing the services; and whether the fee is fixed or contingent.

Rule: The fee must be reasonable. Factors for measuring reasonableness are:

1. Time and labor.
2. Novelty and difficulty.
3. Skill required.
4. Likelihood that representation will preclude other employment if apparent to the client.
5. Local customary fee.
6. Amount involved.
7. Results obtained.
8. Time limitations imposed by client or circumstances.
9. Nature of professional relationship.

10. Length of professional relationship.
11. Experience.
12. Reputation.
13. Ability of lawyer.
    *Fixed or contingent fee.
    **Other factors applicable to the particular representation.

A better outline looks like this:

Rule: The fee must be reasonable. Factors for measuring reasonableness are:

1. the nature of the particular task required;
2. time and labor required;
3. novelty and difficulty of the questions involved;
4. skill requisite to perform the legal service properly;
5. time limitations imposed by the client or the circumstances;
6. amount involved;
7. likelihood of preclusion of other employment, if apparent to the client
   a. likelihood of preclusion
   b. whether apparent to the client;
8. professional characteristics of the lawyer
   a. lawyer's experience
   b. lawyer's ability;
9. the results obtained;
10. the fees customary for similar services in the locality;
11. whether the fee is fixed or contingent;
12. the nature and length of client's professional relationship with lawyer.

APPENDIX B

✟

ISSUE IDENTIFICATION

EXERCISE 1

Amina, a supervisor at the Community Center, threatened to quit unless her salary was increased. The director of the center orally offered a 10 percent increase each year for two years. The director mailed a contract to Amina with those provisions. Amina signed the contract but did not mail it back. She worked at the new salary until she was fired without cause. In the breach of contract action she brought against the Community Center, the center claimed that no binding contract existed. The applicable rules are as follows:

1. An offeree must notify the offeror of acceptance of the offer.
2. The Statute of Frauds provides that a service contract for more than one year must be in writing in order to be enforceable.

A. Under the Statute of Frauds, was the offeree's failure to deliver the signed contract to the offeror an invalidation of the agreement?
B. Under the Statute of Frauds, did the employee notify the employer of acceptance when the mode of acceptance was not specified and she continued to work at the salary increases contained in the offer, but did not mail a copy of the signed contract to the employer?
C. Under the Statute of Frauds, was the offeree required to give notice of acceptance?

D. Under the Statute of Frauds, did a contract exist between the offeror and the offeree when the offeree failed to notify the offeror of acceptance of the offer?

EXERCISE 2

At the intersection of Main and Broad Streets in Princeville, the defendant, Jobari, ran a red light in order to avoid being struck in the back by a speeding vehicle. He collided with another vehicle being driven by the plaintiff, Akil. Jobari was driving a 1998 Ford and Akil was driving a 1979 Honda. Akil was injured and his car was totaled. The applicable rules are as follows:

1. It is unlawful to drive through a red light.
2. A person is liable for injuries or property damages caused by her negligence.

A. Under the law of negligent operation of automobiles, was the driver of a 1998 Ford, which strikes an older Honda being driven by another, totaling it and injuring the other driver, liable to the other driver if the collision between the two vehicles was caused by the driver who ran the red light?
B. Under the law of negligent operation of automobiles, is the driver of an automobile who illegally runs a stop light negligent?
C. Under the law of negligent operation of automobiles, is Jobari, who ran a red light and collided with Akil, liable for injuries and property damages sustained by Akil as a result of the collision, when Jobari ran the red light to avoid being struck in the back by another vehicle?
D. Under the law of negligent operation of automobiles, is Jobari liable to Akil for negligence, which caused the accident in which Akil sustained injuries?

EXERCISE 3

Issue Identification and Formulation

RULE

If any person shall possess any property, money, or other valuable thing, such person knowing or having reasonable grounds to believe the same to have been feloniously stolen or taken, he shall be guilty of a felony if he intends to permanently deprive the owner of the item.

FACTS

Alexis was taking her teenage daughter, Mona, to school one morning after her ex-husband, Chauncey, had returned their daughter from a monthly visitation weekend. Mona was very excited. She said, "Mom, I stole this check from daddy. That is what he gets for not paying child support." Alexis took the check and told Mona she was going to return it immediately to Chauncey. The check was for $10,000.00, and it was going to expire within the next seven days, due to the age of the check. Alexis decided to take the check, but placed it in Mona's math book for safekeeping (the place she knew Mona would never look). Alexis did not tell Mona or her ex-husband about the check until the next month, when Chauncey came for his visit. When Chauncey found out that Alexis had intentionally waited until after the check had expired to tell him about it, he was furious. He cannot cash the check because it has expired. He wants to seek relief.

Outline the rule and identify facts that relate to each element of the rule:

ANSWER

If any person
> Alexis is a person

shall possess
> Alexis put the item in Mona's math book. She never physically kept the check.

any property, money or valuable thing
> The check was of value. It was worth $10,000.00.
> Such person

knowing or
> Alexis knew Mona took the check.

having reasonable grounds to believe
> Mona told Alexis that she stole the check.

the same to have been feloniously stolen or taken
> Mona told Alexis that she stole the check.

he shall be guilty of a felony
> Alexis took the check and intended to keep it from Chauncey until it expired.

if he intends to permanently deprive the owner of the item

Alexis kept the check away for only a month. However, after the month was over, the check had expired.

Identify which elements are at issue.

Answer: shall possess

AND **if he intends to permanently deprive the owner of the item**.

EXERCISE 4

RULE:

No agreement limiting the rights of any person to do business anywhere in North Carolina shall be enforceable unless such agreement is in writing and duly signed by the party who agrees not to enter into any such business.

FACTS

Mohammed Shahid-El is a very successful businessman in Oxford, North Carolina. He has operated several businesses, including Oxford Luxury, LLC, a laundry service that picks up clients' clothes from their homes or work and returns the clothing the next day to the desired address. Mr. Shahid-El has operated this business in Oxford for over 20 years. There is no other company that performs this same service in Oxford. Mr. Shahid-El likes the fact that there is no competition for his business. He services Oxford and all surrounding counties.

Based upon the advice of his lawyer, Mr. Shahid-El has placed a covenant not to compete in his employee handbook. The covenant not to compete reads as follows:

> *No employee of Oxford Luxury, LLC may operate a laundry service within a 100 mile radius of Oxford, N.C. (to include N.C. and VA. territories) for at least 10 years from the termination of the employment relationship with Oxford Luxury, LLC.*

The handbook is about 15 pages long. He gives a handbook to all employees at their orientation. Each employee must sign the last page of the handbook to acknowledge receipt of the handbook. The acknowledgement reads as follows:

> *I, _____, do hereby acknowledge receipt of this employee handbook. I further acknowledge that Oxford Luxury, LLC is not offering me a fixed contract for employment because the employment is subject to the will and desire of the company.*

This is a contract as long as it is signed and agreed to by the parties. I agree to abide by the terms in this employee handbook based on my reading and understanding of the terms.

A few months ago, Mr. Shahid-El hired a legally blind employee, Mike Jones. Mr. Shahid-El gave Mike all of the new employee materials, including the employee handbook. Mike told Mr. Shahid-El that his mother is his power of attorney, meaning that she is legally authorized to engage in certain transactions for him, including the signing of contracts. Mike took all of the paperwork to his mother to review and sign. She signed all of the documents as Mike's power of attorney.

Recently, Mr. Shahid-El fired Mike for singing and trying to make rap songs while he was supposed to be at work. A week later, Mike Jones started his own laundry delivery service in Danville, Virginia (approximately 25 miles from Oxford, NC). Mr. Shahid-El has written Mike a cease-and-desist letter, demanding that he close the laundry business because it is in violation of the contract he had with Oxford Luxury, LLC. Mike has written a response, advising Mr. Shahid-El that he was unaware of any such agreement and intends to continue operating his business.

Outline the rule and identify facts that relate to each element of the rule:

No agreement

The document states that it is a contract, but only if it is signed and agreed to by the parties.

limiting the rights of

Mike Jones was limited in his ability to compete with Mr. Shahid-El.

any person

Mike is a person.

to do business

The agreement was regarding a covenant not to compete with a laundry business.

anywhere in North Carolina

Mike Jones' business was located in Virginia.

shall be enforceable UNLESS

such agreement is in writing

The agreement, if any, was in writing.

duly signed

Mike Jones' power of attorney signed the documents for him.

by the party who agrees not to enter into any such business.

Mike Jones did not sign the employee documents. His POA signed on his behalf. Identify which elements are at issue.

Answer: No agreement
AND by the party who agrees not to enter into any such business.

APPENDIX C

Ψ

OBJECTIVE MEMORANDUM

*Note: These samples were written by first- and second-year law students. The examples are not necessarily perfect; however, they represent strong efforts.

Sample 1

INTEROFFICE MEMORANDUM OF LAW

TO: Professor
FROM: Jamie Wilkerson
RE: Dee Black and Fast Cash Mortgage Company
DATE: November 25, 2008

ISSUES

The issue is whether Dee Black may bring an action against Fast Cash Mortgage Company for violation of the North Carolina Anti-Predatory Lending Act as a borrower pursuant to N.C. Gen. Stat. § 24-2 if: (1) Dee's mother Cee had a one-half interest in the home that was used as security for the loan; (2) Dee is now a co-owner of the property after inheriting the one-half interest in it from Cee; (3) Cee signed the Deed of Trust acknowledging that the home was encumbered by the loan; and (4) Eddi, Cee's "special friend," was the only one to sign the promissory note for the loan.

is whether Cee received a reasonable net, tangible benefit from the loan N.C. Gen. Stat § 24-10.2 (c) if: (1) a portion of the loan was used to pay off the existing $15,000.00 mortgage on the home which was two months behind at the time; (2) Eddi received $59,000.00 in cash from the loan; (3) a portion of the cash received from the loan was used to pay off Cee's credit card for $1,500.00; (4) Eddi used a portion of the loan proceeds to purchase a new stove for Cee for $500.00; (5) $1,000.00 of the loan amount was used to pay property taxes on the home; (6) the original mortgage had a fixed rate of 5 percent; and (7) the new loan taken out from Fast Cash was an adjustable rate mortgage that started at 4.8 percent, adjustable every six months up to 15 percent.

FACTS

On May 1, 2006, Cee Black gave her friend, Eddi, a one-half interest in her home to allow Eddi to take out a loan on the property. The home still had $15,000.00 remaining on the mortgage and the interest rate was fixed at 5 percent. On May 2, 2006, Eddi took out a loan from Fast Cash Mortgage Company for $75,000.00 at an interest rate of 4.8 percent, adjustable every six months up to 15 percent. The home was only valued at $60,000.00. Eddi signed the promissory note, but Cee signed the Deed of Trust, acknowledging that her home was encumbered by the loan. Fifteen thousand dollars of the new loan was used to pay off the existing mortgage, which was two months behind. One thousand dollars from the loan was used to pay property taxes on the mortgaged property. Eddi received $59,000.00 in cash at the loan closing, which she used to pay off Cee's credit card bill for $1,500.00, to purchase a new stove for Cee for $500.00, and to make a down payment on a new home in Cary. Eddi later moved in with Cee, who passed away. Dee Black, Cee's daughter and the sole benefactor in Cee's estate, inherited Cee's one-half interest in the home. The loan balance was $74,000.00. Eddi stopped making mortgage payments three months ago, and foreclosure proceedings are currently pending on the home. Eddi asked Dee to pay half of the monthly mortgage. Dee does not think that she should be obligated to pay half of the $74,000.00 mortgage, and she would like to file an action against Fast Cash for loan flipping in violation of the North Carolina Anti-Predatory Lending Act.

ANALYSIS

Dee should be able to bring an action against Fast Cash Mortgage Company as a borrower under N.C. Gen. Stat. § 24-2. N.C. Gen. Stat. § 24-2 provides that "if security has been given for an usurious loan and the debtor or other person having an interest in the security seeks relief against the enforcement of the security … the debtor or other person having an interest in the security shall be entitled to damages[.]" N.C. Gen. Stat. § 24-2 (2008). The statute may be interpreted broadly to consider a person who has a co-ownership in the security as a borrower even if he/she did not sign the promissory note. *Id.*

One case on point with this issue is *Wally v. Homeaway Financial Network*, 400 B.R. 181 (Bankr. E.D.N.C. 2007). Alice Wally was the co-owner of a home in Garner with her daughter Theresa, and they were both obligated by a debt on the residence. *Wally v. Homeaway Financial Network*, 400 B.R. 181 (Bankr. E.D.N.C. 2007). On October 3, 2002, Theresa refinanced the debt. *Id.* at 182. Alice did not sign the promissory note, but she did sign the Deed of Trust and Notice of Right to Rescission. *Id.* The defendant sought to foreclose on the home. *Id.* Alice filed an adversary proceeding against the defendants pursuant to N.C. Gen. Stat. § 24-10.2 (c) alleging loan flipping. *Id.* The defendant filed a motion to dismiss arguing that N.C. Gen. Stat. § 24-10.2 (c) only applies to a borrower and that Alice was not a borrower. *Id.* The court denied the motion to dismiss and held that Alice had standing to pursue relief under N.C. Gen. Stat. § 24-2 as a borrower. *Id.*

Like the mother and daughter in *Wally*, both Dee and Alice are co-owners of the property used as security for the loan. Dee inherited her ownership interest in the home from her mother, Cee. Also, as in *Wally*, where Alice did not sign the promissory note, neither Dee nor Cee signed the promissory note. Only Eddi signed the promissory note. Despite the fact that Alice did not sign the promissory note, the court in *Wally* allowed her to bring an action as a borrower.

However, in *Wally*, Alice signed the Deed of Trust. While Dee's mother, Cee, signed the Deed of Trust, Dee did not. The court in *Wally* stated that N.C. Gen. Stat. § 24-10.2 (c) "may be enforced by 'any party to a consumer home loan' which may be broad enough to encompass a signatory to the deed of trust who is not an obligor on the note." *Wally* at 182. Also, while Dee spent her childhood in the home in Monroe, she does not currently live there, although she does wish to retire there. In contrast, the court in *Wally* pointed out that Alice Wally had lived in the home for forty years, and she was currently living there. *Id.* Finally, Alice was an original co-owner in the home, whereas Dee inherited her co-ownership interest.

Based on these facts, Dee should be able to bring an action against Fast Cash as a borrower. Even though she did not sign the promissory note and does not currently live in the home, her mother, Cee, signed the deed of trust, and she inherited her mother's interest in the home.

Next, Dee will show that Cee did not receive a reasonable net, tangible benefit from the loan. N.C. Gen. Stat. §24-10.2 (c) provides that

> No lender may knowingly or intentionally engage in the unfair act or practice of "flipping" a consumer home loan. Flipping a consumer home loan is the making of a consumer home loan to a borrower which refinances an existing consumer home loan when the new loan does not have reasonable net, tangible benefit to the borrower considering all of the circumstances, including the terms of both the new and refinanced loans, the cost of the new loan, and the borrower's circumstances.

N.C. Gen. Stat. § 24-10.2 (c) (2008).

The Bankruptcy Court for the Eastern District of North Carolina discussed the issue of whether a reasonable net, tangible benefit had been received from a loan in *Homeowner v. Ohno Federal Mortgage*, 270 B.R. 170 (Bankr. E.D.N.C. 2005). In *Homeowner*, Judy Homeowner refinanced an existing mortgage on her home to get a lower interest rate and to get money for home improvements. *Id.* at 172. Judy's original loan was a two-year adjustable rate mortgage which started at 8.5 percent. *Id.* She executed a promissory note, using her home as security for the new loan, an adjustable rate mortgage, which started at 8.0 percent. *Id.* Judy never missed a payment, and was never late with her payments. *Id.* Judy received a $30,000.00 cash distribution at the loan closing, and added a new room onto her property. *Id.* Later, the mortgage interest rate adjusted three times in two years to 10.0 percent. *Id.* Judy argued that she would have to pay $62,000.00 in additional interest over the life of the loan, putting her in a worse financial position compared to the previous loan. *Id.* As such, she argued that she did not receive a reasonable net, tangible benefit from the loan. *Id.* The defendant moved to dismiss the action based on the allegations that the loan produced no benefit for the borrower and filed a motion to dismiss. *Id.* The court declined to dismiss the cause of action, stating that it was not clear whether $62,000.00 was a fair payment for $30,000.00. *Id.* The court pointed out that under N.C. Gen. Stat. § 24-1, the new loan must be better than the old one to qualify as having a reasonable net, tangible benefit. *Id.*

In both Dee's situation and in *Homeowner*, the new mortgage had an adjustable rate that adjusted more rapidly than the original mortgage. Also, in both situations, the new mortgage started at an interest rate that was lower than the original mortgage. Finally, in both Dee's situation and in *Homeowner*, a lump sum of cash was distributed at the loan closing.

However, in *Homeowner*, the original mortgage was not behind. *Homeowner* at 172. Under the present facts, the original mortgage was two months behind. Another distinction is that in *Homeowner*, both mortgages had an adjustable rate, but Cee's original mortgage had a fixed rate, while the new mortgage had an adjustable rate. Finally, in *Homeowner*, Judy received all of the cash distributed at the loan closing. *Id.* In contrast, Cee did not receive any cash from the subject loan. Eddi received the cash proceeds from the loan, but a portion of the cash was used to pay off Cee's credit card bill, buy her a stove, pay off her existing mortgage, and pay the property taxes due on the home.

Based on these facts, Dee would likely be able to show that Cee did not receive a reasonable net, tangible benefit from the new loan. The new loan was not better than the old loan, as the new loan had an adjustable rate, while the old loan had a fixed rate. The public policy discussed in *Homeowner* may help Dee even further. The court in *Homeowner* noted that when looking at Judy's claim, it was important to take into account that Judy was an unsophisticated and uneducated borrower. *Homeowner* at 172. The court stated that loan transactions involving adjustable rate mortgages may sometimes be confusing to a borrower who is not necessarily knowledgeable about real estate transactions. *Id.*

CONCLUSION

Dee has a strong case against Fast Cash for loan flipping. She will likely be able to show that she qualifies as a borrower under N.C. Gen. Stat. §24-2, and that under all the circumstances surrounding the new loan, Cee did not receive a reasonable net, tangible benefit. Public policy serves to protect borrowers who are unsophisticated or uneducated and who enter into real estate transactions unaware of the consequences that arise when a mortgage has adjustable rates.

SAMPLE 2

INTEROFFICE MEMORANDUM OF LAW

TO: Managing Partner
FROM   Jordan Ford
RE: Potential Embezzlement Case
DATE: November 24, 2009

ISSUES PRESENTED

The issue is whether, pursuant to N.C. Gen. Stat. §14-90, Mr. Bally received Ms. Jennings's first monthly payment to Medical Collections Corporation (MCC) as an exercise of his fiduciary duty when: (1) Mr. Bally was authorized to receive debtors' first payment to MCC by paper check; (2) Mr. Bally was not authorized to remove cash from any MCC account; (3) Ms. Jennings voluntarily gave Mr. Bally her money through the monthly arrangement with MCC; (4) Ms. Jennings told Mr. Bally to treat the collections call as a friend-to-friend communication; (5) Ms. Jennings mailed her first payment to MCC to Mr. Bally's home address; (6) Ms. Jennings made the check payable to Mr. Bally in care of MCC; and (7) Mr. Bally used the money toward his wife's surgery.

The issue is whether, pursuant to N.C. Gen. Stat. § 14-90, Mr. Bally fraudulently misapplied to his own use Ms. Jennings first monthly payment to MCC when: (1) Mr. Bally applied credit to Ms. Jennings's account when it should not have been credited; (2) Mr. Bally was not authorized to remove cash from any MCC account; (3) Ms. Jennings proposed that Mr. Bally take her first payment to MCC; (4) Ms. Jennings sent a paper check to Mr. Bally's home with his name and address on the envelope; (5) Ms. Jennings made the check payable to Mr. Bally in care of MCC; and (6) Mr. Bally intended to put the money back into his company's account as soon as he could.

STATEMENT OF FACTS

Mr. Bally worked as a collections employee for Medical Collections Corporation (MCC). His duties included calling debtors to encourage them to pay their medical bills and setting up payment plans for those who could not pay in full. While the debtor's first payment had to be by paper check, the remaining payments were to be debited automatically from a checking account provided by the debtor. Mr. Bally's wife was in need of emergency surgery, but his insurance only covered 60 percent of the cost. When Mr. Bally called Ms. Jennings because she owed money to a cancer treatment center, he told her about his own dilemma. After agreeing to make monthly payments to MCC, Ms. Jennings proposed that Mr. Bally take her first monthly payment to help pay for his wife's surgery. Ms. Jennings told Mr. Bally that she was voluntarily giving him the money and to treat the collections call as a friend-to-friend communication. Mr. Bally received Ms. Jennings's first monthly payment to MCC in the form of a paper check addressed to him in care of MCC at his home address. Mr. Bally then applied the money toward his wife's surgery. However, he intended to put the money back in his company's account as soon as he could. Sometime after Ms. Jennings had successfully paid off her collection bill, Mr. Bally's supervisor fired him for embezzlement. Mr. Bally now seeks the advice of this firm to see if he is likely to be convicted of embezzlement.

DISCUSSION

Mr. Bally is likely to be convicted of embezzlement. N.C. Gen. Stat. § 14-90 provides that "[i]f any person exercising a fiduciary duty … shall embezzle or fraudulently … misapply … any money … belonging to any other person or corporation … which shall have come into his possession or under his care, he shall be guilty of a felony." N.C. Gen. Stat. § 14-90 (2009). A defendant may be convicted of embezzlement when that "defendant's possession of property was obtained in the normal course of his employment." *State v. Weaver*, 207 N.C. App. 309, 310 (2007). Furthermore, the State need only show that the defendant "fraudulently misapplied the property for purposes other than those for which she received it as agent or fiduciary." *State v. Dickerson*, 124 N.C. App. 200, 209 (2005). The defendant's intent to defraud may be reasonably inferred through facts and circumstances. *Id.*

In *State v. Weaver*, the defendant, Mr. Weaver, was indicted on twelve counts of embezzlement, each alleging that he aided and abetted Kimberly, his former wife. *Weaver*, 207 N.C. App. at 309. Kimberly's duties at R & D included balancing the company's bank statements, recording monthly inventory reports, and recording the monthly profit-and-loss statement. *Id.* However, "she had no general check writing authority." *Id.* at 309. While working for R & D, Kimberly obtained blank checks from two different corporate bank accounts. *Id.* Using her employer's signature stamp without permission, Kimberly forged over twenty checks for her own personal use. *Id.*

In *Weaver*, Kimberly's testimony demonstrated that she did not come into possession of the checks or her employer's signature stamp lawfully within the terms of her employment. *Id.* at 310. The court held that the defendant was therefore not guilty of aiding and abetting Kimberly's alleged embezzlement, explaining that a "defendant cannot be convicted of aiding and abetting embezzlement without proof that an embezzlement was committed." *Id.* at 310.

The duties of both Mr. Bally and Kimberly involved some form of interaction with the financial records of their employers. Also, both Mr. Bally and Kimberly misappropriated funds from their respective employers' accounts. Finally, neither Mr. Bally nor Kimberly had the proper authority to remove any cash from the company's accounts.

In *Weaver*, Kimberly had no authority to possess or write checks. *Id.* Mr. Bally, however, was authorized to receive debtors' first monthly payment to MCC by paper check. Kimberly used her employer's signature stamp without permission to forge over twenty checks. *Id.* In contrast, Ms. Jennings voluntarily gave her first check to MCC to Mr. Bally instead. In *Weaver*, Kimberly used her employment with R & D to obtain blank checks from two separate accounts. *Id.* Unlike Kimberly, Mr. Bally obtained Ms. Jennings' money through what was considered a friend-to-friend communication. Kimberly obtained the blank checks while at work. *Id.* Mr. Bally, on the other hand, received Ms. Jennings' first payment to MCC at his home address. While Kimberly wrote unauthorized checks to herself, Ms. Jennings made her check payable to Mr. Bally in care of MCC. *Id.*

Based on the facts, it is likely that a court will determine that Mr. Bally's actions occurred in the course of his employment with MCC. Mr. Bally was authorized to receive debtors' first payment to MCC by paper check, and did so when he accepted Ms. Jennings' check made payable to him, in care of MCC. Although Mr. Bally applied Ms. Jennings' check toward his wife's surgery, his initial receipt of her first monthly payment was within the terms of his employment. *Id.*

In *State v. Dickerson*, Ms. Dickerson worked as an accounts receivable clerk for Pate-Dawson. *Id.* After noticing several problems with bank reconciliations for accounts handled by Ms. Dickerson, Pate-Dawson terminated her employment. *Id.* A review of Ms. Dickerson's records, while at Pate-Dawson, revealed cash received by Ms. Dickerson that did not appear on any deposit slips to the bank. *Id.* Ms. Dickerson, without authorization, had applied bank credits to customer accounts that should not have been credited. *Id.* Altogether, forty-five similar instances were identified, and negative entries found in certain accounts handled by Ms. Dickerson on more than 100 days. *Id.* After detectives searched Ms. Dickerson's home, they discovered numerous stacks of paper bearing Pate-Dawson accounting information. *Id.* Ms. Dickerson was indicted on one count of embezzlement. *Id.*

In order to uphold a conviction of embezzlement, the State only needed to show that the defendant "fraudulently misapplied the property for purposes other than those for which she received it as agent or fiduciary." *Id.* at 201. The court held that the State provided evidence of Ms. Dickerson's "fraudulent misapplication or conversion of money," and affirmed the trial court's denial of Ms. Dickerson's motion to dismiss the embezzlement charges. *Id.*

Both Mr. Bally and Ms. Dickerson managed the accounts of their employer's customers. Mr. Bally and Ms. Dickerson misapplied money belonging to their respective employers. Specifically, Mr. Bally and Ms. Dickerson each applied credit to a customer's account that should not have been credited, allowing cash to be removed without it showing in the company's accounting documentation. Neither Mr. Bally nor Ms. Dickerson had the proper authority to remove any cash from the company's customer accounts.

In *Dickerson*, Ms. Dickerson removed cash from the company's accounts on her own accord. *Id.* On the contrary, Ms. Jennings came up with the idea that Mr. Bally take her first monthly payment to MCC. Ms. Dickerson's home was discovered to contain numerous stacks of paperwork bearing Pate-Dawson accounting information. *Id.* Mr. Bally received one payment from Ms. Jennings at his home address. In *Dickerson*, Ms. Dickerson removed cash without any showing on the register she submitted to Pate-Dawson. *Id.* Ms. Jennings, however, made her check payable to Mr. Bally in care of MCC. Furthermore, Ms. Dickerson applied credit to forty-five accounts that should not have been credited, compared to the single account to which Mr. Bally applied an unauthorized credit. *Id.* In *Dickerson*, Ms. Dickerson's records showed over 100 days with negative entries on "paid on account" logs, indicating she had no intent to replace the funds she had removed from the Pate-Dawson accounts. *Id.* Mr. Bally, on the other hand, intended to put the money back in his company's account as soon as he could.

Based on these facts, Mr. Bally's actions are likely to be considered fraudulent. Although Mr. Bally used Ms. Jennings's money for his wife's surgery with the intent to repay MCC, he misapplied Ms. Jennings's property for purposes other than those for which he received it as an agent or fiduciary.

CONCLUSION

Mr. Bally is likely to be convicted of embezzlement. Mr. Bally's actions were within the scope of his fiduciary duty and his application of Ms. Jennings' first payment was fraudulent in nature. If the State can prove these two elements, Mr. Bally is likely to be convicted.

SAMPLE 3

To: Senior Partner
From: Intern
Date: 10 April 2010
RE: Rule 41 Issue in *Homeowners' Association v. Group Home Facility*

Issue:

Our client, Homeowners' Association, wishes to appeal from orders dated 20 December 2004 by Judge Charles Brown and 21 February 2005 by Judge Marcy Green. To support its appeal, Plaintiff sets forth one assignment of error.

Procedural History:

In June 2004, Judge Charles Brown conducted a trial on Plaintiff's motion for a preliminary injunction to keep Defendant from allegedly violating community covenants. Judge Brown denied Plaintiff's motion on 20 December 2004.

A non-jury trial on the merits was conducted by Judge Marcy Green in February 2005. At trial, Plaintiff's evidence tended to show that Plaintiff is a large planned-unit subdivision with approximately 2,350 homes. Gaye Black, Defendant's community manager, testified that Homeowners' Association's residents complained that the operation of the Group Home Facility, which was a property within the Homeowners' Association community, was in violation of community covenants. The Group Home Facility is owned by Defendant HLG Builders, Inc., and was being leased to Children's Homes.

Facts:

The Group Home Facility is a group-home facility that operates out of a single-family home. The Group Home Facility is licensed by the N.C. Department of Health and Human Services through the Division of Facility Services. George Lee, an employee of Children's Homes, which is now defunct, testified that Children's Homes was a company that provided 24-hour care in a residential setting for children with developmental disabilities. Prior to becoming defunct, Children's Homes leased the Group Home Facility on a month-to-month basis. Children's Homes paid a monthly rent to Matthew Hunter. After Children's Homes became defunct, Mr. Lee took over the residential supervision duties and operated the business as Hunter Homes. Hunter Homes now operates four separate residential group homes.

On more than one occasion, police officers were called to the Group Home Facility. However, Mr. Lee was never informed why. Mr. Lee testified that it is protocol to call the police should a minor leave the residential home for longer than fifteen minutes. In addition, protocol requires that a hospital be called if a resident attempts to hurt himself.

Hunter Alternative, a for-profit organization, bills Medicaid $232.36 on a daily basis for Group Home Facility, as it is a Level 3 facility. At the Group Home Facility, residents are only accepted by doctors' orders.

In addition to the above evidence, Plaintiff offered the following exhibits: (1) Exhibit 1A, the Fifth Amendment to Declaration of Covenants, Conditions, and Restrictions for Homeowners' Association; (2) Exhibit 1B, Registration and Licensure Documents for Group Home Facility; (3) Exhibit 1H, Contract between Wake County and Hunter Homes, Inc. for the term of 1 July 2003 to 30 June 2004; (4) Exhibit 1I, Addendum #1 to Contract between Wake County and Hunter Homes, Inc.; and (5) Exhibit 1T, County Index of Mental Health Facilities Licensed by the Division of Facility Services of the N.C. Department of Health and Human Services.

In the Covenants, Article XII, Section 24, is titled, "Business Use." It provides, in pertinent part:

> [N]o trade or business may be conducted in or from any Unit, except that an Owner or occupant residing in a Unit may conduct business activities within the Unit so long as: (a) the existence or operation of the business activity is not apparent or detectable by sight, sound or smell from outside the Unit; (b) the business activity conforms to all zoning requirements for the Properties; (c) the business activity does not involve persons coming on to the Properties or door-to-door solicitation of residents of the Properties; and (d) the business activity is consistent with the residential character of the Properties and does not constitute a nuisance, or hazardous or offensive use, or threaten the security or safety of other residents of the Properties, as may be determined in the sole discretion of the Board.

> The terms "business" and "trade", [sic] as used in this provision, shall be construed to have their ordinary, generally accepted meanings, and shall include, without limitation, any occupation, work or activity undertaken on an ongoing basis which involves the provision of goods or services to persons other than the provider's family, and for which the provider receives a fee, compensation, or other form of consideration, regardless of whether: (i) such activity is engaged in full or part-time; (ii) such activity is intended to or does generate a profit; or (iii) a license is required therefore. Notwithstanding the above, the leasing of a Unit shall not be considered a trade or business within the meaning of this section.

Exhibit 1A, pp. 40-41. Section 27 is titled, "Leasing of Units." It provides the following:

(a) Definition. "Leasing", [sic] for purposes of this Declaration, is defined as regular, exclusive occupancy of a Unit by any person or persons other than the Owner for which the Owner receives any consideration or benefit, including, but not limited to a fee, service, gratuity, or emolument.

(b) Leasing Provisions.

(i) General. Units may be rented only in their entirety; no fraction or portion may be rented. There shall be no subleasing of Units or assignment of leases unless prior written approval is obtained from the Board of Directions. [sic] No transient tenants may be accommodated in a Unit. All leases shall be in writing and shall be for an initial term of no less than six (6) months, except with the prior written consent of the Board or Directors. Notice of any lease, together with such additional information as may be required by the Board, shall be given to the Board by the unit [sic] Owner within ten (10) days of execution of the lease. The owner must make available to the lessee copies of the Declaration, By-Laws, and the rules and regulations. The Board may adopt reasonable rules regulating leasing and subleasing.

(ii) Compliance with Declaration, By-Laws and Rules and Regulations. Every Owner shall cause all occupants of his or her Unit to comply with the Declaration, By-Laws, and the rules and regulations adopted pursuant thereto, and shall be responsible for all violations and losses to the Common Areas caused by such occupants, notwithstanding the fact that such occupants of a Unit are fully liable and may be sanctioned for any violation of the Declaration, By-Laws, and rules and regulations adopted pursuant thereto.

After the presentation of Plaintiff's evidence, Defendant moved for a Rule 41 dismissal. After hearing arguments from both parties, the trial judge granted Defendant's motion and dismissed Plaintiff's claims pursuant to Rule 41(b) of the N.C. Rules of Civil Procedure.

Discussion:

Where there is a trial by the court, sitting without a jury, the appropriate motion by which a defendant may test the sufficiency of plaintiff's evidence to show a right to relief is a motion for involuntary dismissal pursuant to Rule 41(b) of the N.C. Rules of Civil

Procedure. *Vernon v. Lowe*, 148 N.C. App. 694, 559 S.E.2d 288, *rev'd on other grounds*, 356 N.C. 421, 571 S.E.2d 584 (2002). Rule 41(b) provides, in pertinent part

> For failure of the plaintiff to prosecute … a defendant may move for dismissal of an action or of any claim therein against him. After the plaintiff, in an action tried by the court without a jury, has completed the presentation of his evidence, the defendant, without waiving his right to offer evidence in the event the motion is not granted, may move for a dismissal on the ground that upon the facts and the law the plaintiff has shown no right to relief. The court as trier of the facts may then determine them and render judgment against the plaintiff or may decline to render any judgment until the close of all the evidence. If the court renders judgment on the merits against the plaintiff, the court shall make findings as provided in Rule 52(a). Unless the court in its order for dismissal otherwise specifies, a dismissal under this section and any dismissal not provided for in this rule, other than a dismissal for lack of jurisdiction, for improper venue, or for failure to join a necessary party, operates as an adjudication upon the merits.

N.C. Gen. Stat. § 1A-1, Rule 41(b) (2005).

Plaintiff's claim against Defendant was for violation of residential covenants. In order for a restrictive covenant to be binding against subsequent purchasers of land, it must be in writing and duly recorded. *Miles v. Carolina Forest Ass'n*, 167 N.C. App. 28, 34, 604 S.E.2d 327, 331 (2004). There was ample evidence presented at trial in the exhibits that the restrictive covenants complained of by Plaintiff were in writing and recorded.

The aforementioned covenants prohibited owners from business use. However, the covenants allowed a home to be used as a business where the operation of the business activity is not apparent, the business activity is properly zoned, the business does not involve door-to-door solicitation, and the business activity is consistent with the residential character of the Properties and does not constitute a nuisance, or hazardous use, or threaten the security or safety of other residents of the Properties.

Plaintiff believes that Hunter Homes' operation is inconsistent with the residential character of Homeowners' Association. Judge Green found as fact that the Group Home Facility is "a residential facility for children and adolescents who have a primary diagnosis of mental illness or emotional disturbance[.]" In addition, Judge Green noted that George Lee had testified that the Group Home Facility "provides only room, board, and transportation services for the residents." Judge Green concluded that the Group Home Facility maintained a residential character. Plaintiff has not provided evidence to show that the Group Home Facility was not in conformity with the residential character of the Homeowners' Association community. Mr. Lee testified that some residents run businesses out of their homes, but only if there is not excessive coming and going from the home or excessive parking problems along the street. Indeed, there was no evidence presented that these problems existed at the Group Home Facility.

Plaintiff believes that the safety of neighbors was being compromised because of the problems of the Group Home Facility residents. In particular, Plaintiff testified about one instance in which the police had been called to the Group Home Facility. However, Plaintiff did not produce any evidence as to why the police had been called and did not explain whether the incident involved a safety issue at all.

Plaintiff also alleges that the 21 February 2005 Order is problematic because of issues regarding licensing, public policy, and the for-profit characterization of the Group Home Facility. However, none of these factors is a basis for Plaintiff's complaint. After a careful review of the orders from which Plaintiff has appealed, the trial court likely did not abuse its discretion. *See Clark v. Clark*, 301 N.C. 123, 129, 271 S.E.2d 58, 63 (1980).

Conclusion:

Plaintiff will likely be unsuccessful in its appeal.

APPENDIX D

STATUTORY INTERPRETATION EXERCISES

EXERCISE D-1

To:	**Summer Associate**
From:	**Senior Partner**
Date:	**October 3, 2006**
RE:	**Potential Citizen-Taxpayer Suit Challenging School Transportation Supplement**

I have been approached to represent a group of elderly citizens who are looking for ways to trim the county budget of "local pork." They resent that special interests groups have been so successful in lobbying elected officials that, as they see it, some luxury programs are drawing scarce funds from basic programs which benefit everyone.

They are considering filing a lawsuit to challenge the county's "School Transportation Subsidy." This county program pays a school transportation subsidy directly to private schools so that children who attend those schools can ride shuttle buses if they live more than two miles from their chosen school. Upon receiving a signed agreement that the school will use the funds to provide or contract for the provision of transportation to benefit school-aged children, the county manager pays the schools a fixed amount at the beginning of the year. The schools, most of which are operated by the Catholic archdiocese, make the actual transportation arrangements. This direct payment method is handled by the county manager's office pursuant to a local fiscal regulation concerning county spending from the county's general fund "for lawful purposes." The general fund and the school transportation subsidy are completely separate from the school district's fleet of yellow buses, which are paid for out of education funds and administered by the school district. In the past, funds were available to public schools to supplement field trips and extracurricular activities, but that practice ceased because of the county's budget problems.

At a meeting last night at the county-operated Senior Center, one especially active member, Mr. Wainwright, recounted that when he was a child, he used to ride a public school bus to his Methodist elementary school but that some law made the county stop supporting religious education. Another member, Mrs. Porter, mentioned that she remembers how the judges helped the colored community when she was child by prohibiting the school district from forcing colored families to accept public school buses to the one colored elementary school, while it built numerous elementary schools in white neighborhoods. She said all that was of no use by the time her children came along because by then everybody got bused to schools all over the county.

I came across an article by a local historian who confirms these stories in the bigger context of the county's struggle to use publicly subsidized transportation to support and enforce compulsory attendance laws. According to the article, the state supreme court did find in 1942 that providing public transportation to children attending parochial schools violated the state constitution. *Sherrard v. Jefferson County Board of Education*, 294 Ky. 469, 171 S.W.2d 963, 967 (1942). After Sherrard, the 1944 legislature enacted a new statute, KRS 158.115, which expressly permits counties to supplement school transportation for children attending school in compliance with compulsory attendance laws. Subsequently, *Nichols v. Henry* upheld KRS 158.115 as constitutional on its face. 301 Ky. 434, 191 S.W.2d 930 (1945).

I meet with the group again next week and would like to advise the group generally whether the county's school transportation subsidy is legal under the state statute KRS 158.115 and county regulation 67.080. Since it appears that the county fiscal regulation allows the county to appropriate money for "lawful purposes" and compulsory school attendance is clearly a lawful purpose, I want you to focus on whether the means by which the county is providing the supplement is legal. Please address the following:

1) Use language from KRS 58.115(1) to make the argument that the county's payment to private schools exceeds its discretion.

Model Response: The discretion to supplement school transportation from the general fund is limited by the word "all." If the county chooses to provide school transportation under KRS 58.115 (1), the supplement must benefit "all pupils" required to attend school. The Jefferson County school transportation supplement only benefits children who attend private schools but not children who attend public schools. Therefore, the Jefferson County school transportation supplement illegally exceeds the county's discretion.

2) Apply the expressio unius est exclusio alterius canon of construction to KRS 158.115(2). Make the argument that the legislature did not intend payments directly to private schools.

Model Response: Applying the canon of *expressio unius est exclusio alterius*, which means the expression of one thing is the exclusion of another, the legislature did not intend a county to make payments to private schools for transportation expenses. The legislature listed specific means of acceptable supplemental transportation, not including direct payments. Therefore, the legislature intended to authorize only the listed means.

Exercise D-2

Calvin was a simple man who loved monkeys. He spent his entire life training monkeys how to sing and dance hip hop, jazz, and country music numbers for tips on the streets of Warsaw, North Carolina. During the economic downturn, it became hard for Calvin to get his monkeys to get the really good tips. He bought the cutest outfits and created the most elaborate choreographed dances for the monkeys. However, the monkey dancing business did not improve. Calvin noticed that his monkeys were gaining weight. They were consistently gaining weight, even though Calvin had cut back on their food supply. Calvin was concerned about the monkeys' excess weight because nobody wants to see lethargic monkeys dance.

One day, Calvin looked at the monkeys and they were scratching at his knees, which was their usual sign that they wanted to run around the streets for some free play. Calvin released the monkeys from their chains and told them they could run around the neighborhood for thirty minutes. Ten minutes later, Braxton came up to Calvin and punched him in the throat. Braxton yelled, "I'm tired of your monkeys eating my freaking caviar. They have eaten a jar everyday for the last five days. Each jar costs $200.00, and you are going to pay me back or I will kick the snot out of you and eat your monkeys."

The District Attorney wants to prosecute for a felony charge of possession of stolen goods for stealing Braxton's caviar under § 14-71.1. Calvin intends to plead not guilty to the charges because he did not steal the caviar. Calvin acknowledges that the monkeys were under his exclusive control. He also acknowledges that he owns the monkeys.

The only applicable statute is as follows:

§ 14-71.1 Possessing Stolen Goods

a. If any person shall possess any property, goods, money or other valuable thing, such person knowing or having reasonable grounds to believe the same to have been feloniously stolen or taken, he shall be guilty of a felony.

b. The value of the item stolen shall be at least one thousand dollars ($1,000.00) or greater.

1. Use mischief rule canon to argue that Calvin is the "person" responsible for stealing the caviar.

a. Define the Mischief Rule.
b. Explain how the rule of law applies to the facts.
c. Identify the key facts in the problem.
d. What conclusion can you draw?

2. Use the Plain Meaning Rule to argue that if Calvin is charged for a crime, he should not be charged with a felony.

a. Define the Plain Meaning Rule.
b. Explain how the rule of law applies to the facts.
c. Identify the key facts in the problem.
d. What conclusion can you draw?

ANSWER:

Mischief Rule—statute is to be read in the light of some assumed purpose or objective.

Analysis—applies the rule to the facts in an organized manner and develops a solid argument. (Calvin is a person. He did not steal the caviar. Calvin's monkeys stole the caviar, but they are not people. If Calvin is not charged with the crime, it will go unpunished. The statute was designed to convict people of crimes. Calvin's monkeys are his responsibility and he can be found guilty of the crime as the person responsible for the animals.)

Key facts: Calvin owned the monkeys. Calvin was not aware that the monkeys were stealing. However, Calvin let the monkeys run free in the park. Calvin noticed the monkeys were gaining weight, even though their food supply was limited.

Conclusion: Calvin can be charged for the felony. While he is not the one who has stolen the items, he is the one who is responsible for the animals who stole the items.

Plain Meaning Rule—if there is no ambiguity within the text, the plain meaning of the statute must be followed.

Analysis—applies rule to facts in an organized manner and develops a solid argument.

Key facts: The caviar was worth $200.00 per jar. The monkeys only stole one jar at a time over a five-day period. While the cumulative value of the stolen caviar was $1,000.00, the statute references only one item and not an accumulated value.

Conclusion: The charge cannot be a felony because none of the individual jars of caviar was worth $1,000.00 or greater.

APPENDIX E

✝

SYNTHESIS PRACTICE

EXERCISE E-1

Case 1

This case only involves one issue: whether the banana goes into the basket. After careful consideration, we determine that it does. Whether green or yellow, a banana is a soft fruit which easily could be damaged if left unprotected. Accordingly, the trial court acted properly in finding that it should go in the basket.

Case 2

The coconut, still in its shell, stays out of the basket. Its weight would adversely impact the basket and preclude placing any other object in the basket. Accordingly, we affirm the trial court's judgment finding that the coconut stays out.

Case 3

The trial court acted correctly in excluding the green cucumber from the basket. The cucumber is bumpy and slick and does not belong in the basket. Moreover, it is a vegetable, and only fruits, to date, have been permitted in the basket.

Case 4

The orange does not go in the basket, as the trial court correctly found. The orange, brightly colored, will be noticed by customers even without the additional adornment the basket provides.

Fashion a rule from these cases individually.

Case	1	2	3	4
Facts				
Holdings				
Legally Significant Factors				
Rules				

Finding the General Principle

Case 1

This case only involves one issue: whether the banana goes into the basket. After careful consideration, we determine that it does. Whether green or yellow, a banana is a soft fruit which easily could be damaged if left unprotected. Accordingly, the trial court acted properly in finding that it should go in the basket.

Case 2

The coconut, still in its shell, stays out of the basket. Its weight would adversely impact the basket and preclude placing any other object in the basket. Accordingly, we affirm the trial court's judgment finding that the coconut stays out.

Case 3

The trial court acted correctly in excluding the green cucumber from the basket. The cucumber is bumpy and slick and does not belong in the basket. Moreover, it is a vegetable, and only fruits, to date, have been permitted in the basket.

Case 4

The orange does not go in the basket, as the trial court correctly found. The orange, brightly colored, will be noticed by customers even without the additional adornment the basket provides.

Fashion a rule from these cases individually.

Case	Fact	Holding	Legally significant factors	Rule
1	Banana	In	Soft fruit, easily damaged if left unprotected	Soft fruits, i.e., those which could be easily damaged if left unprotected, go in
2	Coconut	Out	In shell, weight would adversely impact basket; precludes placing other items into basket	Weighty (and large) items, which adversely impact the basket and preclude placing other objects in the basket, stay out.
3	Green cucumber	Out	Bumpy and slick, a vegetable; only fruits (to date) have been permitted in the basket	Bumpy and slick non-fruit items stay out.
4	Orange	Out	Brightly colored, noticeable by customers, no need for adornment basket provides	Brightly colored items that will be noticed by customers without the additional adornment the basket provides stay out.

General principle

The general principle from these cases is that soft fruits, such as bananas, which need the basket's protection, go in. However, weighty and large items, such as a coconut in its shell, which could adversely impact the basket and preclude placing other objects into the basket, stay out. Bumpy and slick non-fruit items, such as cucumbers, also stay out; as do brightly colored oranges, which customers will notice without the additional adornment the basket provides.

Synthesis of the four cases

The appearance, shape, and weight of a fruit determine whether it should go into the basket. In Case 1, the court held that soft fruits that need protection should go in the basket. On the other hand, in Case 2, the court noted that heavy fruits or fruits encased in a protective shell do not need to be in the basket. Indeed, including heavy or large items would preclude other items from going into the basket. Additionally, as stated in Case 4, brightly colored fruits need not go in the basket because they do not need the additional adornment that the basket would provide, unlike yellow or green fruits. Unlike the products in Cases 1, 2, and 4, vegetables do not go into the basket; only fruits have been included in the past.

Exercise E-2

Amanda worked for her husband's business, Make It Do What It Do, Inc., a non-pork based chitterling manufacturer. Gary, Amanda's husband, claimed that he used very expensive lean turkey to make the chitterling concoction. The business was in high demand and the couple did very well financially.

In November 2008, the Food and Drug Administration began an investigation into the authenticity of the company's product. Gary knew his business would be ruined if the public found out that there was really no way to make non-pork based chitterlings and the company has always been using fat back and hog jowls to make the product. Gary decided to write a big check to a political candidate in hopes that this would stop the FDA investigation. This investigation could ruin his business, so Gary instructed his wife to donate their entire life's savings to the political candidate's campaign. Amanda never asked Gary why he was making such a big donation. She just thought he really liked that candidate. Unfortunately for Gary, an unlikely candidate won the election and the investigation continued.

In January 2009, Gary decided to tell Amanda about the problems the company was facing. Gary decided that he would secretly take the money from the employees' retirement accounts and try to bribe Dr. Ponce, the new head of the FDA. Dr. Ponce was presented with a briefcase full of $1.5 million in exchange for discontinuing the investigation into the products used to make the non-pork based chitterlings. Dr. Ponce took the money, but demanded $2.5 million more. Gary asked his wife to help him fix the books so the employees would not see that their retirement accounts were depleted. Amanda agreed. She created fake reports, and convinced the employees and the accountants that everything was in order.

Ultimately, Dr. Ponce took the money and fled the country. When the FDA investigation continued, Gary's business was exposed as a fraud. When the employees went to cash out their retirement accounts, they discovered there was no money available. Gary pled guilty to misdemeanor fraud. Amanda has been charged with accessory before the fact to felony embezzlement, felony embezzlement, and accessory after the fact to felony embezzlement. She was convicted of all three charges and wants to know if she can appeal.

Read the following cases:

State v. Lattimore

Defendant and his brother worked at a local store called Priscilla's. Defendant's brother, Cee-Cee, was the manager. Cee-Cee routinely took bras and panties from the store without paying for them. Defendant never stole any items from the store. One day, Cee-Cee decided to take 75 bras and 112 panties from the store in a brown Piggly Wiggly Grocery Store bag. As Cee-Cee was taking the items to his car, Defendant saw the owner of the store coming toward Cee-Cee. Defendant grabbed the bag from Cee-Cee and ran out the door in an effort to prevent Cee-Cee from getting caught. The owner contacted the police. After a quick investigation, the police found thousands of stolen bras and panties at Cee-Cee's home. The police also recovered a brown Piggly Wiggly Grocery Store bag from Defendant that contained 74 bras and 111 panties. Apparently, Cee-Cee was wearing the missing set. Cee-Cee was charged with multiple felonies, but ultimately pled guilty to a lesser misdemeanor charge. Subsequently, Defendant was charged as an accessory before the fact for felony employee embezzlement. The case went to trial and Defendant was found guilty. Defendant appeals.

The defendant assigns error to the denial of his motion to dismiss the charge of felony employee embezzlement. The defendant was tried as an accessory before the fact after the principal had pled guilty to a lesser charge of misdemeanor appropriations of funds. He contends he could not be tried for any greater offense than the offense to which the principal pled guilty, which was misdemeanor appropriation of funds.

In *State v. Arnold*, 329 N.C. 128, 404 S.E.2d 822 (1991), we held it was reversible error to submit second-degree murder to the jury in the case of an accessory before the fact to murder. We held that only first-degree murder should have been submitted. *Arnold* holds that an accessory before the fact may be tried for first-degree murder, although the principal has pled guilty to second-degree murder. The same rule applies to Defendant. Evidence of another defendant's plea does not take away the culpability of the defendant in the case at bar if the crime committed was felonious in nature. Thus, defendant was properly charged and convicted.

This assignment of error is overruled.

State v. Sanders

On or about 21 March 2007, Bradley Hicks (Mr. Hicks) successfully gained illegal access to the UNC–Chapel Hill Student Grades Database. This database allowed Mr. Hicks the ability to change grades for any student enrolled at UNC. Mr. Hicks was able to achieve this felonious accomplishment without any help. He would break into the Registrar's Office every night to access the database. On or about 29 March 2007, the UNC Registrar, Camilla Sanders (Defendant), came back to her office after hours and saw Mr. Hicks leaving. Defendant asked Mr. Hicks what he was doing in her office. Mr. Hicks admitted that he had committed a crime by accessing the UNC Student Grades Database. Defendant advised Mr. Hicks that she would assist him in keeping his crime undetected if he gave her $5,000.00. Mr. Hicks complied. Subsequently, if anyone at UNC would ask her about students who told them about errors on their transcripts, Defendant would say it was a computer error and she would then change the grades back. An investigation ensued, and Mr. Hicks was arrested. He pled guilty to a felony computer tampering charge. Defendant was charged with the same felony computer hacking charge, and Defendant was charged with accessory after the fact because she covered up the crime for Mr. Hicks.

Defendant now appeals. After careful review, we vacate the judgment and order a new trial.

Defendant first argues that the trial court erred in failing to instruct the jury that it could only convict defendant of felony computer hacking or accessory after the fact to computer hacking, but not both.

At trial, defendant made no objections to the jury instructions that allowed the jury to consider both charges. Accordingly, defendant has not preserved this assignment of error. However, defendant has requested plain error review.

> [T]he plain error rule ... is always to be applied cautiously and only in the exceptional case where, after reviewing the entire record, it can be said the claimed error is a *fundamental error*, something so basic, so prejudicial, so lacking in its elements that justice cannot have been done," or "where [the error] is a grave error which amounts to a denial of a fundamental right of the accused," or the error has "'resulted in a miscarriage of justice or in the denial to appellant of a fair trial'" or where the error is such as to "seriously affect the fairness, integrity or public reputation of judicial proceedings" or where it can be fairly said "the instructional mistake had a probable impact on the jury's finding that the defendant was guilty."

State v. Odom, 307 N.C. 655, 660, 300 S.E.2d 375, 378 (1983) (quoting United States v. McCaskill, 676 F.2d 995, 1002 (4th Cir. 1982)).

Defendant was charged with felony computer hacking based on the theories of acting in concert and aiding and abetting, and being an accessory after the fact to felony computer hacking. "The acting in concert doctrine allows a defendant acting with another person for a common purpose of committing some crime to be held guilty of a felony committed in the pursuit of that common plan even though the defendant did not personally commit the felony." State v. Roache, 358 N.C. 243, 306, 595 S.E.2d 381, 421 (2004).

"An accessory after the fact is one who, knowing that a felony has been committed by another, receives, relieves, comforts or assists such felon, or who in any manner aids him to escape arrest or punishment." *State v. Oliver,* 302 N.C. 28, 55, 274 S.E.2d 183, 200 (1981).

The trial court in the present case properly allowed both charges to go to the jury. However, the crux of this case is whether the trial court was *required* to instruct the jury that defendant could only be convicted of the principal felony of felony computer hacking *or* of being an accessory after the fact to felony computer hacking. The State contends that the trial court is not required to give such an instruction; rather, the court is required to arrest judgment on the accessory after the fact conviction if the defendant is convicted of both crimes, which is the action the court took in this case. *Jewell* did not address this specific issue. In *Jewell,* the defendant pled guilty to being an accessory after the fact to murder and the murder charge was dismissed; therefore, a jury trial never occurred. *Id.* at 351, 409 S.E.2d at 758.

Futher, given the peculiar posture in which this case comes before us, we conclude that there is a "reasonable possibility" that a different result would have been reached at trial as to both charges, *had the trial court correctly instructed the jury that it could convict the defendant only of one offense or the other, but not of both.* Therefore, the defendant is entitled to a new trial on both charges. *Id.* at 580, 391 S.E.2d at 168 (internal citations omitted) (emphasis added).

We further hold that the error was not cured by the trial court's decision to arrest judgment on the accessory after the fact conviction. If properly instructed, the jury might have determined that defendant was guilty of accessory after the fact to murder and not guilty of the murder itself. We decline to substitute our judgment for that of the jury.

In the present case, defendant was convicted of two mutually exclusive crimes that carried substantially different penalties and collateral consequences. Again, we cannot substitute our judgment for that of the jury and hold that the trial court should have arrested judgment on the felony computer hacking conviction. Given the proper instruction, the jury might have found defendant guilty of felony computer hacking and not accessory after the fact. Accordingly, we find that *Hall* is not controlling here.

We hold that the trial court committed plain error in failing to instruct the jury that it could convict defendant of felony computer hacking or accessory after the fact to felony computer hacking, but not both. Because we cannot substitute our judgment for that of the jury, we vacate the judgment and order a new trial.

1. What is the general principle that you derived from the cases?

2. What were the legally significant facts in *State v. Lattimore*?
3. What was the holding in *State v. Lattimore*?
4. What were the legally significant facts in *State v. Sanders*?
5. What was the holding in *State v. Sanders*?
6. What were some significant comparisons and contrasts between *State v. Sanders*, *State v. Lattimore*, and the present situation?
7. What conclusion would you reach based on your synthesis of the cases?

Answers:

General Principle: A defendant can be charged as an accessory before the fact to a felony when the principal has pled to a lesser charge. A defendant cannot be convicted of both the main offense and an accessory after the fact to the main offense as long as they arose from the same incident.

Key facts in *State v. Lattimore*: Cee-Cee pled guilty to a misdemeanor charge. Defendant was charged and convicted of a felony.

Holding in *State v. Lattimor*: Defendant was properly charged with accessory before the fact to a felony when the principal was convicted of a lesser charge.

Key facts in *State v. Sanders*: Defendant was charged with accessory after the fact and the underlying charge. The jury convicted Defendant of the underlying felony charge and as an accessory after the fact

Holding in *State v. Sanders*: It was improper to instruct the jury to consider both charges, but not to instruct the jury that Defendant could only be guilty of one charge.

Case discussion

In *Lattimore* and the present situation, the principals were convicted of a lesser offense than the person who was charged with accessory before the fact. In both cases and the present situation, the Defendants were motivated to engage in criminal conduct by third parties. Unlike the defendants in *Lattimore* and *Sanders*, Amanda was charged with accessory before the fact and accessory after the fact.

Conclusion

A defendant can be charged as an accessory before the fact to a felony when the principal has pled to a lesser charge. A defendant cannot be convicted of both the main offense and an accessory after the fact to the main offense as long as they arose from the same incident. Amanda can be charged with accessory before the fact to the felony, even though the principal has pled guilty to a lesser charge. It was an error for Amanda to have been found guilty of the accessory after the fact and the underlying charge. The jury should have been instructed that they can only find her guilty of either the principle offense or accessory after the fact, not both.

APPENDIX F

✝

PERSUASIVE MEMORANDUM

IN THE CIRCUIT COURT OF THE FIRST JUDICIAL CIRCUIT, IN AND FOR TANDY COUNTY, FLORIDA

Case No.: 09-CRS-1234
Division: Criminal

STATE OF FLORIDA
V.

AMANDA LEWIS,
Defendant

MEMORANDUM IN OPPOSITION TO DEFENDANT'S MOTION TO SUPPRESS

INTRODUCTION

Defendant Amanda Lewis (hereinafter "Defendant") was arrested for various drug-related offenses after a search and seizure of her vehicle revealed the presence of certain contraband. Prior to trial, defendant filed a motion to suppress that contraband seized during the search alleging that the search and seizure of her vehicle was illegal. The State is requesting that the Court deny Defendant's motion to suppress for the foregoing reason: The officer had reasonable suspicion to justify the initial stop and sufficient probable cause to search the entire vehicle, including the trunk.

FACTS

On January 15, 2009, Officer J.T. Gattis, a police officer with fifteen years of experience, was at a convenience store when he was approached by a store customer. The customer informed the officer that two girls inside the store smelled of marijuana and alcohol, and that she was 100 percent sure of this because the two girls stood beside her while she was in the store. After pointing out the two girls to the officer, the customer left. Although the customer failed to give the officer her name, she was a regular shopper at the store, whom Officer Gattis had seen on more than one occasion. The two girls identified were the defendant, Amanda Lewis and her friend, Erica.

The officer followed the girls as they left the convenience store and stopped their vehicle. When the defendant rolled down the driver's side window of the vehicle, Officer Gattis suspected that he smelled marijuana emanating from the car, and he noticed that the passenger's eyes were red. The defendant refused the officer's request to search the vehicle, but he proceeded with the search. Upon searching the vehicle, the officer found a black bag containing syringes, vials of Depo-Testosterone, and a small bag of marijuana. The defendant immediately informed the officer that the contraband was hers. She was arrested and charged with possession of marijuana. She filed a motion to suppress the seized contraband, asserting that the stop was invalid, and that the search producing the contraband was illegal. The defendant explained that the passenger's eyes were red because she was studying for the LSAT and not because she had consumed marijuana.

ARGUMENT

INVESTIGATORY STOP WAS VALID BASED UPON REASONABLE SUSPICION

The investigatory stop made by Officer Gattis was valid based on reasonable suspicion generated by the tip from the convenience store customer. A police officer is justified in making an investigatory stop when he has reasonable suspicion that such action is warranted. *Terry v. Ohio*, 392 U.S. 1 (1968). Reasonable suspicion is comprised of "specific and articulable facts which, taken together with rational inferences from those facts, would warrant a man of reasonable caution in the belief the one factor that may give rise to reasonable suspicion justifying an investigatory stop is a tip from an informant such as the store customer. Supporting this principle, the Supreme Court held in *Alabama v. White* that an informant's tip may carry sufficient "indicia of reliability" to justify an investigatory stop. *Alabama v. White*, 496 U.S. 325 (1990). The tip does not have to be sufficient to support an arrest or a search warrant, but must be corroborated by independent police work. *Id.* at 330.

Despite the fact that the convenience store customer did not provide her name or other information when she gave the tip, she is not automatically to be deemed as an anonymous informant. The holding of *State v. Evans* provides that an informant cannot be deemed anonymous if his/her identity is readily ascertainable. *State v. Evans*, 692 So.2d 216 (Fla. Dist. Ct. App. 1997).

In *Evans*, the manager of McDonald's noticed that the defendant, who was a customer in the drive-thru line, appeared to be intoxicated. *Id.* at 218. The defendant was incoherent, fumbling to get the food, and had dilated eyes. *Id.* The manager also smelled alcohol. She called the police, gave her name, address, location, and occupation. *Id.* She provided a description of the defendant's vehicle and tag number. *Id.* The officer, who received the tip from the dispatcher and did not know the caller's name, arrived at McDonald's. *Id.* The manager pointed at the defendant's vehicle which matched the information the officer received from the dispatcher. *Id.* The officer pulled the vehicle over after the defendant left McDonald's. *Id.* The officer noticed that the defendant smelled of alcohol, and after failed performance tests, the officer arrested the defendant. *Id.* A search of the vehicle revealed beer and packages of marijuana. *Id.* The defendant was charged with driving under the influence of alcohol, resisting arrest, and possession of marijuana with intent to sell. *Id.*

In the case at bar and *Evans*, both defendants were pulled over by an officer, but had not violated any traffic law. Despite the fact that the defendant in *Evans* was not pulled over for a traffic violation, the court upheld the validity of the stop. As such, the fact that the defendant in the instant case had not violated any traffic laws prior to being stopped should not have any bearing on the validity of the stop made by Officer Gattis. Both cases involved a stop made based on a tip from an informant who smelled a substance on the defendant, notified an officer, and made a positive identification of the individual to the officer. Also, upon stopping the vehicle, both officers smelled substances that were in line with what was stated in the informant's tip.

In contrast, the informant in *Evans* gave her name, address, location, and occupation when she called the dispatcher. However, the informant does not have to provide a name or address at the time that the tip is given so long as the officer has some way of later ascertaining the informant's identity. *Id.* at 219. Here, Officer Gattis knows that the customer is a regular shopper at the convenience store, has seen her on prior occasions, and can easily ascertain her name and any other identifying information.

Furthermore, not only is the customer's identity readily ascertainable, but she would qualify as a citizen informant, as defined by the court in *Evans*, thus making her tip even more reliable. A citizen informant is one who is motivated not by pecuniary gain, but by the desire to further justice. *Id.* Such a tip is placed at the high end of the tip-reliability scale. *Id.* The convenience store customer did not stand to receive any pecuniary gain when she approached the officer to apprise him of the fact that she smelled marijuana on the two girls. Her only goal was to alert the officer of prospective criminal activity in an effort to further justice.

Courts have also held that a face-to-face tip given by an informant who has not given identifying information is presumed to be inherently more reliable than an anonymous telephone tip because the officers receiving the information have an opportunity to observe the demeanor and perceived credibility of the informant. *U.S. v. Heard,* 367 F.3d 1275 (11th Cir. 2004). In *Heard,* an officer was apprised of a fight in the train station by several patrons. Id. at 1277. The defendant and an unidentified woman were fighting in the train station. The officer disrupted the fight and made the defendant pay the unidentified woman money that he owed her. Id. As the officer and the woman were leaving the station, the woman informed the officer that the defendant was carrying a gun. *Id.* The officer turned back to approach the defendant, telling the woman to remain to give a statement. *Id.* She got on the train and left, never to be seen again. *Id.* The officer conducted a frisk of the defendant and found a gun. *Id.* The defendant was charged with possession of a firearm and sought to have the evidence suppressed, arguing that the officer did not have reasonable suspicion based on the tip because the tip was from an unreliable anonymous source. *Id.*

The instant case and *Heard* are analogous on a point that was dispositive to the court's ruling in *Heard.* Both tips were given by individuals who were face-to-face with the officer when they gave the tip, although neither informant provided the officer with identifying information. Officer Gattis had the opportunity to observe the demeanor and perceived credibility of the convenience store customer when she gave him the tip. As a fifteen-year law enforcement veteran, Officer Gattis would be seasoned enough to determine whether the customer was a reliable party and whether her demeanor would indicate something other than a genuine interest and desire to further justice.

In addition, there is one distinction between the instant case and *Heard* which is actually favorable to the State's case: the informant in *Heard* was someone the officer had never seen before, unlike in the case at bar where the officer had seen the customer on prior occasions. It is critical that the court upheld the reliability of the tip from the informant in Heard despite the fact that she was not someone the officer had ever seen before.

While there are some cases that provide that a tip from an anonymous informant is not sufficient to generate reasonable suspicion for a stop, those cases are not applicable to our set of facts. One such case is *Solino v. State* where the court held that the anonymous tip from the informant was insufficient to provide reasonable suspicion justifying an investigatory stop because the informant could not be identified and the information was not corroborated. *Solino v. State,* 763 So.2d 1249 (Fla. Dist. Ct. App. 2000).

In *Solino*, an anonymous passing motorist flagged down an officer and informed him that someone in the defendant's vehicle had thrown a bottle out of the window of the vehicle. *Id.* at 1250. The motorist then drove off without providing identifying information, and the officer did not obtain the license tag number from the vehicle of the informant. *Id.* Furthermore, the officer did not see the bottle thrown and he did not attempt to locate the bottle. *Id.* Instead he stopped the vehicle, demanded identifying information from the defendant who initially lied about his identity. *Id.* After learning of the defendant's identity the officer made a computer check and discovered that the defendant's license was suspended and that he was in violation of probation on a prior conviction of burglary. *Id.* The officer attempted to arrest the defendant who fled from the scene. *Id.* The defendant later argued that the officer lacked sufficient reasonable suspicion to justify the stop. *Id.*

While both *Solino* and the case at bar involve a tip from an individual who did not provide the officer with identifying information, there are significant distinctions. In *Solino*, the informant merely informed the officer that a bottle had been thrown out of a vehicle window. This information is not enough to warrant a man of reasonable caution to believe that an investigatory stop is necessary. In addition, the officer failed to corroborate the information contained in the tip. In contrast, Officer Gattis stopped the defendant's vehicle and performed an independent investigation. These distinctions make *Solino* inapplicable to the facts of the present case.

Officer Gattis, in his discretion, did not question the customer's basis of knowledge in detecting the scent of marijuana. However, such a decision is consistent with the principle of *White* that an informant tip used in the reasonable suspicion context requires a lesser showing than what is necessary for making an arrest. *White*, 496 U.S. at 329. Therefore, it was not necessary for the officer to determine the customer's basis of knowledge in detecting the scent of marijuana before making the stop.

In conclusion, Officer Gattis had sufficient reasonable suspicion, based on the tip from the convenience store customer, to justify the investigatory stop he made of the defendant's vehicle. The convenience store customer qualifies as a citizen-informant, and the fact that the tip was given face to face, places her tip at the high end of the tip-reliability scale. Moreover, the tip was appropriately accompanied by police corroboration.

SEARCH OF VEHICLE BASED UPON PROBABLE CAUSE WAS VALID

The search made by Officer Gattis was valid based upon probable cause generated by the customer's tip, the passenger's red eyes, and the smell of marijuana emanating from the vehicle. Pursuant to *Illinois v. Gates*, the test for determining whether probable cause exists to conduct a search based on a tip from an informant is the totality of the circumstances. *Illinois v. Gates*, 462 U.S. 213 (1983). Probable cause means a "fair probability that contraband or evidence of a crime will be found." *Id.* at 238.

Admittedly, the tip standing alone is insufficient to justify probable cause for a search and must be corroborated by independent police investigation. However, using the tip from the convenience store customer as a means of making the investigatory stop of the defendant's vehicle, further investigation by the officer revealed circumstances that would give rise to a fair probability that contraband or evidence of a crime would be found in the defendant's vehicle.

First, the officer detected the smell of marijuana emanating from the vehicle when he approached the vehicle and the defendant rolled down the window. During this time the officer also noticed that the passenger's eyes were red. These two factors taken together would warrant the reasonable man to believe that contraband, perhaps marijuana, would be found in the vehicle.

Once the officer has ascertained that there is a probability that the vehicle may contain contraband, he may conduct a warrantless search of the vehicle. The Supreme Court held in *United States v. Ross* that once probable cause exists of the possibility of contraband being in the vehicle, the officer may conduct a search as thorough as a magistrate could authorize by warrant. *United States v. Ross*, 456 U.S. 798 (1982). Thus, "if probable cause justifies the search of a lawfully stopped vehicle, it justifies the search of every part of the vehicle and its contents that may conceal the object of the search." *Id.* at 825. It flows naturally from this holding that the officer's authority to search the entire vehicle includes the authority to search the trunk. The smell of marijuana justified the search of the stopped vehicle, and as such, it justified a search of every part of the vehicle.

The holding in *State v. Betz*, reiterates this point. The court held that where the smell of marijuana emanates from the interior of the vehicle, there exists probable cause to search the entire vehicle, including the trunk. *State v. Betz*, 815 So.2d 627 (Fla. 2002).

In *Betz*, the defendant was stopped because the left headlight of his vehicle was not working. *Id.* at 629. The officer smelled the odor of marijuana emanating from the vehicle, saw gray smoke in the car, and smelled marijuana on the defendant's shirt. *Id.* The officer patted down the defendant and found a plastic bag of marijuana. *Id.* He arrested the defendant, searched the trunk, and found a second bag of marijuana. *Id.* The court determined that based upon the totality of circumstances within the perception of the law enforcement officers, probable cause existed to search the entirety of the defendant's vehicle. *Id.* The defendant made a motion to have the evidence suppressed. *Id.*

The instant case is analogous to *Betz* on an issue that was significant to the court's ruling. The officers in both cases detected the odor of marijuana emanating from the interior of the vehicle and ultimately found marijuana in the trunk of the vehicle. In contrast, in *Betz*, there was smoke in the vehicle, and the smell of marijuana also emanated from the defendant's person. *Id.* Finally, the officer in *Betz* found a small bag of marijuana on the defendant's person. *Id.* Despite the existence of these distinctions, the deciding factor in the validity of the search's scope was the odor of marijuana emanating from the vehicle. The smell of marijuana allowed the officer to extend the search to the trunk. *Id.* The other factors that were present in *Betz* are not required in every case and such factors will vary depending on the facts and circumstances of each situation. The court must look at the totality of the circumstances and the perception of the officer at the time of the stop. The factors in Officer Gattis' perception when he stopped the defendant's vehicle were sufficient to provide probable cause to search the entire vehicle.

In conclusion, probable cause to search the entire vehicle, including the trunk, existed because Officer Gattis was justified in believing that there was a probability that contraband would be found in the vehicle based on the tip, the smell of marijuana, and the passenger's red eyes.

CONCLUSION

The weight of the authority presented justifies the court's denial of the defendant's motion to suppress the contraband found in her vehicle. The officer had sufficient reasonable suspicion based upon the tip from the customer, coupled with corroboration, to justify the investigatory stop. Based on the totality of the circumstances—the customer's tip, the smell of marijuana, the passenger's red eyes—the officer had sufficient probable cause to conduct a search of the entire vehicle, including the trunk. Therefore it follows that the stop was valid, the search was valid, and any evidence produced from the search was not illegally obtained and should not be suppressed.

Respectfully submitted,
Jamie Wilkerson

APPENDIX G

✝

ENGAGEMENT LETTER

Example G-1

The Williams Group
1512 S. Alston Avenue
Durham, North Carolina 27707
Phone: (919) 484-9279
Fax: (919) 484-4045
www.thewilliamsgroup.com

Sam Thompson
1234 Jones Street
Durham, N.C, 2701
(919) 897-3556
February 2, 2009

RE: Engagement Letter

INTRODUCTION

Dear Mr. Thompson:

Thank you for coming to see Attorney Williams on January 26, 2009. I am Jamar Creech, an associate attorney with The Williams Group. We are pleased that you chose The Williams Group to help you in this initial phase and are very excited to work with you on your possible workers' compensation claim. I hope that you are feeling better and that your injuries are not causing you too much pain. The purpose of this letter is to (1) verify the information previously given to Attorney Williams; (2) detail the scope of our representation; and (3) inform you of the next steps, if you choose to have The Williams Group represent you.

FACTUAL SUMMARY

Based on your initial conversation with Ms. Williams, we summarized all the information you gave us. In order for us to research the claim and properly advise you of your rights, I need you to verify the following information. If there are any discrepancies, please let me know as soon as possible.

In 2000, while employed at Badtreads (you have been with the company for about twenty-four years) you began working in the first-stage tire building of the company. Initially, you were working twelve-hour shifts but they were shortened to eight-hour shifts. In an eight-hour shift, you built between 160 and 170 tires. As a first-stage tire builder, you were required to build twice as many tires, although there was less rubber cutting than your previous job as a second-stage builder. In order to make the tires, you had to use a large pair of shears to cut a rubber component called an apex, and another rubber component known as a toe guard. In addition, you had to use a hot knife to cut a rubber component known as a ply. While cutting the pieces for the tire, you gripped the tools in your right hand.

In addition, you had to hand stitch the sidewall on each tire. This required applying a lot of pressure to your right hand as you had to stitch two pieces per tire. There were other components of the tire which placed your hands under pressure. For example, you had to press down the rubber liner in the tire to make sure it is lying flat. Also, you had to press down the ply and the apex to ensure that they were in the appropriate condition for the tire. You had to press seven buttons on your tire building machine with your right hand.

In addition to building between 160 and 170 tires per eight-hour shift, you also had to push heavy equipment with the palms of your hands. This occurred for approximately twenty times per shift. You moved carcass trucks which were on wheels, but weigh about 1,000 pounds.

In April 2001, you first noticed problems with your hands. This was approximately one year after you transferred to your position as a first-stage tire builder. Around April 2006, you noticed that both of your hands would cramp up and go to sleep. Eventually the pain in your right hand went to your wrist and ultimately interfered with your ability to build tires.

After going to the plant dispensary you were referred to Cape Fear Orthopedic Clinic for a surgical evaluation. On July 19, 2007, you saw Dr. James Flanagan at Cape Fear Orthopedic Clinic. Dr. Flanagan diagnosed you with bilateral carpal tunnel syndrome and recommended surgery to remedy the condition.

SCOPE OF REPRESENTATION

At this time, we are conducting the initial research into a possible workers' compensation claim. Following our initial research, we will call you and schedule a follow-up meeting so that we can discuss your rights and options. We are providing you with limited representation. Payment will be based on an hourly rate. Our standard price is $200.00 per hour. Prior to the follow-up meeting, you will receive a bill where the expenses will be listed. Payment is due once the research has been completed and we advise you of your rights and options.

NEXT STEPS

After we have concluded the research, we will schedule a follow-up meeting in order to discuss your options. We are very interested in taking your case; and if hired, we will file a form on your behalf with the North Carolina Industrial Commission.

CONCLUSION

Again Mr. Thompson, we appreciate you contacting The Williams Group and are very interested in taking your case. Please verify the above information so that we may better inform you of your rights and options. If you have any questions, please do not hesitate to contact us. I look forward to working with you in the future.

Best Regards,
Jamar Creech

Example G-2

N.C. Central Law Firm
1512 S. Alston Ave.
Durham, North Carolina 27707
919-929-3905

Mrs. Beatrice Potter
13-B Imperial Garden Apartments
555 Hood Dr.
Shatley Springs, NC 28911

Re: Letter of Representation

September 8, 2009

Dear Beatrice:

It was a pleasure meeting you last week when you came to our office. Again, we are sorry for your loss, but it is our belief that our firm may be able to assist you in resolving the matter in a manner that is satisfactory to you. In this letter you will find a summary of the facts as you presented them, a list of items that we need from you, the scope of our representation, and fee arrangements.

FACTS

You have been a resident of the Imperial Gardens Apartment complex since 1998. The Imperial Gardens Apartment complex is owned and operated by Patrick and Duncan McCloud. During the time that you lived there, you were awarded sole legal and physical custody of your grandson, Peter.

Over the past several years, rival gangs reputedly engaged in turf wars in the apartment complex. In the fall of 2006, you called to notify the apartment office that the parking lot streetlights were not working. During this phone call you spoke with an unidentified woman who promised to relay the message to the landlords. You also informed her that every night large groups of people, mostly men you did not recognize as being tenants, would gather in the parking lot to drink and cause trouble. The men fought and left broken bottles and trash in the parking lot and behind apartment buildings. Following this call, no action was taken to fix the lights or to prevent the groups of people from being disruptive.

In February 2007, several shots were fired, two of which hit a resident's car. This resident, Mr. Hubert Doyle, called Mr. Patrick McCloud to inform him of the incident.

Mr. McCloud responded by saying, "That's what automobile insurance is for. I didn't fire no gun, but I gotta say there's a bunch of you people over there I wouldn't mind seeing shot." Shortly after this conversation, Mr. Doyle wrote a letter to Mr. McCloud, listing all problems that were occurring in the complex: apartment rentals to gang members and drug dealers, noisy gatherings, broken bottles, trash everywhere, overgrown weeds, lack of lighting in the parking lot, and shots being fired by criminals in the parking lot. You and 27 other residents signed the letter which was hand delivered to the apartment office on March 3, 2006. No action was taken.

On December 24, 2007, you took Peter outside to hang Christmas lights around your apartment window. Subsequently you heard gunshots. As you pushed Peter back towards your apartment, he stumbled and fell, bleeding from his shoulder and back. Peter was transported by ambulance to the Mt. Madison Medical Center where he died three hours later from gunshot wounds.

In the emergency room you became hysterical and fainted. You suffered a heart attack and were admitted to the cardiac care unit. You were hospitalized for four days and treated for your heart condition, hypertension, and acute depression. Once you were released from the hospital, you were referred to Dr. Freud at the Madison County Adult Mental Health Clinic. Dr. Freud diagnosed you as having acute situational depression and post traumatic stress syndrome, for which she prescribed Zoloft. You are also taking Altace and Norvasc to control your hypertension. On February 10, 2009, you were appointed by the Clerk of Court as the administratrix of Peter's estate. Peter was survived by you, his mother, and his great uncles.

Detective John Adams determined that Peter had been shot by a stray bullet during a gunfight between Ben Cripp and Adam Redding. Cripp was charged for the murders of Peter and Adam, and he was convicted of both charges in August 2009.

The police records of Shatley Springs reveal that the police department has responded on numerous occasions to reports of gunfire in and around your apartment complex. After each incident, the police department forwarded a copy of the incident report to Patrick McCloud. The following is a list of the recorded incidents:

1. September 12, 2005: The police investigated a shooting at the Supermart located a quarter mile from the apartment complex.
2. February 2, 2007: The police investigated the gunfire that resulted in the damage to Mr. Doyle's vehicle.
3. October 31, 2007: The police investigated a report of gunshots in the vicinity of the apartment complex.
4. December 24, 2007: The police investigated the shooting death of Peter and Adam Redding.
5. February 14, 2009: The police investigated the shooting of Maryetta Marsh, a parole officer, who was shot while visiting a parolee who lived in the apartment complex.

Also, on June 3, 2005, a CP&L representative was severely beaten while trying to disconnect electrical service to an Imperial Garden apartment. Subsequently CP&L issued a district-wide directive that no CP&L employee was to enter the complex for any purpose without a police escort. On May 18, 2006, a chief inspector for the Shatley Springs Housing office inspected the apartment complex. The inspector determined the existence of several unsafe conditions and issued a warning to the McClouds. The inspector met personally with Duncan McCloud and strongly suggested that the McClouds take advantage of the expedited eviction process provided under N.C. Gen. Stat. § 42-59 to evict known criminals from the apartment complex. Duncan McCloud responded by saying, "You know life is tough. Those people are like animals, and mink do eat their young. Let's just let nature take its course. The no-good scalawags will weed themselves out on their own. On the rent they pay, they shouldn't expect the Trump Tower."

On January 26, 2004, Patrick and Duncan McCloud were cited and fined for violating the Shatley Springs Housing Code. The violations: failure to maintain adequate exterior lighting in the apartment complex, failure to prevent accumulation of trash in and around the complex, and creating a health risk to tenants by allowing apartment grounds to be overcome by weeds and debris.

Subsequent to Peter's death, the outside lights at the complex have been repaired, the overgrown weeds have been cut, and twelve known gang members have been evicted. In March 2009, the McClouds hired two security guards to patrol the complex from midnight until 5:00 a.m.

LIST OF ITEMS

The following is a list of items that we need you to bring to the office at your earliest convenience:

1. A copy of the medical bills for Peter
2. A copy of the bills for Peter's funeral expenses
3. A copy of Peter's death certificate
4. A copy of your medical bills and prescription bills
5. A copy of the letter to Mr. Patrick McCloud that was signed by the residents.

SCOPE OF REPRESENTATION AND FEES

In order to determine if any claims are available for you to bring on behalf of yourself and Peter, we must conduct further research. There will be no charge to you for this preliminary research. Once the research is complete, you will receive an opinion letter from us in early October. Provided that there are claims that may be brought, if you wish to continue with having our firm represent you, we will discuss fee arrangements at that time.

We would like to thank you again for coming in to our firm and meeting with us. Please take the time to review the facts as stated in this letter. If there are any facts which are stated incorrectly, or if you have any questions, please feel free to contact us. We look forward to working with you further.

Sincerely,
John Doe

Example G-3

The Excellence Law GROUP, PLLC

Mailing Address   Office Location:
P.O. Box 1234   604 Nelson St.
Durham, NC 27707   Durham, NC 27707

Phone: (919) 530-6333   www.excellencelawgroup.com   Fax: (919) 530-1234

MARY SUE JONES
321 ROONEY COVE
RALEIGH, NC 27613

Dear Mary Sue:

Thank you for selecting The Excellence Law Group, PLLC, to assist you with your legal affairs. My name is Kevin Brockenbrough. I am an attorney at the firm and will be your primary legal counsel. This letter confirms our engagement with you and the nature and scope of the services we look forward to providing you.

You are seeking our legal advice following a divorce from the defendant, Jon Jones. We will represent you from the beginning of the litigation process, until its completion. We will ensure that all of our filings and submissions are in compliance with the laws of the State of North Carolina. We will help you draft responses to the Request for Production of Documents and work to lessen your burden of production. We will prepare a strategy in preparation for litigation. We will organize, assist, and facilitate you in mediation with the Defendant. We will complete any necessary settlement forms. We will represent you, should litigation arise. We will not file or represent you on appeal. However, we will advise you as to whether or not you have a sufficient cause for such an appeal.

The attorneys, associates, and paralegals at The Excellence Law Group, PLLC, take attorney-client privilege very seriously. All written, typed, and oral communication is strictly confidential, and will not be discussed with anyone outside of the firm. To ensure that the attorney-client privilege remains valid, I ask that you refrain from forwarding, carbon copying, faxing, or rendering voice recordings of our communications with outside and/or third parties.

A parent is fit to have sole custody of a minor child if he/she is willing to provide a nurturing environment for those children, and it is in the best interest of that child to be in permanent care of that adult. The Court may establish visitation rights for an adult, if it finds that the adult is fit to do so and it would be in the children's best interests to visit that adult.

A parent owes the duty to provide child support, if they are able bodied and have the means to help with the maintenance and support of minor children. That parent must also share in any medical, dental, optical, and pharmaceutical expenses not covered by insurance.

A dependent spouse may receive post separation support and permanent alimony from an able-bodied spouse to support that dependent spouse and maintain that dependent spouse's standard of living.

The Court may partition or equitably distribute marital property (property accumulated or acquired during the course of the marriage) between two legally separated spouses.

A plaintiff who acts on good faith and cannot meet the defendant on equal financial footing to receive sufficient council, may seek the payment of attorney fees, under the pretense that the defendant caused the litigation.

The length and number of steps in this legal process will be determined by the conduct and desires of the parties involved. Initially, I will need to meet with you in person to discuss the particulars of your case. I will take notes on our discussion, review your documents, and begin constructing a general strategy. After our initial meeting, you will be given a list of documents and/or items that you will need to retrieve and bring to my office in preparation for litigation. Next, the materials will be analyzed by me and Mr. Jones' attorney, and used to construct our negotiation strategies. We will attempt to mediate the situation and seek a favorable settlement. If a settlement is not achieved, we will prepare for litigation. If we are unsuccessful in our first attempt, you may seek to have an appeal granted.

Prior to litigation, we will seek to mediate the communications, between you and Mr. Jones, regarding your complaints. This is an attempt to find a less strenuous common ground between opposing parties, in hopes of avoiding the litigation process and the experience that accompanies it. Mediation provides the optimal environment for negotiation, and usually offers the most amicable resolve.

If mediation has proven unfruitful, we will proceed with litigation. During litigation, each party will present facts and evidence in the light most suitable to their respective arguments and contentions. The judge will make a ruling on your requests based on our presentations. After the judge makes his ruling, the dissatisfied party may seek an appeal, in hopes of achieving the desired outcome.

In order to comply with the Request for Production of Documents, I will need to ask you to bring the following materials: any and all documents relating to the children's schooling and daycare; copies of all banking and credit card statements; leasing and rental agreements from August 22, 2005, to the present; copies of all correspondence between you and someone other than myself, regarding your children or this litigation from August 1, 2004, to the present; copies of all retirement accounts from August 22, 2005, through the present; all romantic correspondence between yourself and anyone other than Mr. Jones from August 1, 2003, to the present; cell phone bills; current résumé; job applications, acceptance letters, and rejection letters for any employment endeavors from August 1, 2004, to the present; all payment stubs or payments from any employment from August 1, 2004, to the present; tax returns from 2004–2006; NC State Bar application; payments toward marital debt since August 22, 2005; copies of all reasonable expenses for you or the children from August 22, 2005, to the present.

We will work to keep out all unnecessarily intrusive and arbitrary documents. However, I ask that you provide everything I asked, regardless of how insignificant it may seem.

A retainer of $7,500.00 is required and payments may be made in three (3) individual installments of at least $2,500.00. Each payment is to be made no more than three (3) months after the last. In addition to the retainer fee, there will be billable time. The firm will give consideration to the legal services to be furnished by Attorney, and Client shall pay Attorney at a rate of **$175.00** per hour. Associates will be billed at **$125.00**. Paralegal time will be billed at **$80.00** an hour.

To affirm that this letter correctly summarizes your understanding of the arrangements for this work, please sign the enclosed copy of this letter in the space indicated and return it to us in the envelope provided.

We appreciate your confidence in us. Please call if you have questions.

Sincerely,
Kevin Brockenbrough

APPENDIX H

✝

OPINION LETTER

Example H-1

Williams Law Firm
1512 S. Alston Avenue
Durham, North Carolina 27707
Phone: (919) 484-9279
Fax: (919) 484-4045
www.williamslawfirm.com

Mr. Sam Thompson
1234 Jones Street
Durham, NC 27701

March 24, 2009

Re: Opinion Letter for Your Workers' Compensation Claim

Dear Mr. Thompson:

I hope that your injuries are healing and that you are patient with the process of your claim. I am Jamar Creech, an associate attorney with the Williams Law Firm. As you requested, I have written this opinion letter about your case. An opinion letter is the attorney's opinion on the likely result of a person's case. In your case, the issue is whether you have a compensable occupational disease under the North Carolina Workers' Compensation Act. A compensable occupational disease is one that allows the employee to recover benefits for injuries resulting from work.

Based on my research, it is my opinion that you will likely be able to recover medical and disability benefits as a result of your employment at Badtreads. You will be able to recover medical and disability benefits because you have a compensable occupational disease under North Carolina law. I made this determination based on the facts of your case and the North Carolina Workers' Compensation Act.

First, I would like to begin by giving a short summary of the facts as I understand them. If there is anything wrong with these facts, please let me know as soon as possible. In April 2001, after being employed at Badtreads for twenty-four years, you began noticing problems with your hands. This was also approximately one year after you transferred to your position as a first-stage tire builder. About five years later, you noticed that both of your hands would cramp up and go to sleep. Eventually the pain in your right hand went to your wrist and interfered with your ability to do your job of tire building. You were referred to the Cape Fear Orthopedic Clinic. On July 19, 2000, Dr. James Flanagan of the Cape Fear Orthopedic Clinic diagnosed you with bilateral carpal tunnel syndrome and recommended surgery to remedy the condition. You have been out of work since September 18, 2008.

Next, I would like to briefly review the workers' compensation process with you. There are several steps to this process. First, the employee is supposed to report the injury to the supervisor. Second, the employee fills out an injury form to send to the North Carolina Industrial Commission. Third, after receiving the injury form, the Industrial Commission will contact the employer about the claim being filed. Fourth, the employer must mail a form in response to the injury form (filed by the employee) to the Industrial Commission. If the employer accepts the claim, then there is no need to go to court. If the employer denies the claim, then there are several options for the employee. The first option is that the employee can try to settle with the insurance carrier. The second option is that the employee can request a hearing. The third option is that the employee can simply do nothing. Please be advised that most workers' compensation cases are settled in mediation. But in this case, Badtreads will likely deny your workers' compensation claim.

In evaluating your claim, the state agency that decides if you have established each of the necessary things for the specific laws to your injuries is the North Carolina Industrial Commission. This state agency is similar to the North Carolina court system. The Industrial Commission will first set up a mediation meeting between you, your employer, and its insurance company regarding the liability and compensation for your injuries. The mediation meeting will determine if the employer was at fault and whether you can get paid for your injuries. Opposite of being in a courtroom, mediation usually takes place at one of the attorney's offices. In this meeting the mediator fills out the settlement agreement. The settlement agreement must be approved by the Industrial Commission. The settlement agreement will be paired with a "clincher agreement" to show that the employee will no longer work for the employer.

Although we are not representing your claim at this point, if you choose to have this firm as your legal representative for your claim, the Williams Law Firm would have the mediation take place in our office. If neither party is in agreement during mediation, then the Industrial Commission will hear your claim and decide on the outcome. If there is no settlement in mediation, then the case goes to the Deputy Commission. If you are not satisfied with the result from the Deputy Commission, then you can appeal to the Full Commission. If you are still not pleased with the result of your case, then you can make an appeal to the North Carolina Court of Appeals.

Under North Carolina law, there are three things that the employee must prove for a compensable occupational disease. First, the disease must be one of which others in the employee's trade or line of business also has a likely chance of catching. Secondly, the disease cannot be one in which every other person outside of the trade or occupation is equally likely to catch. Finally, your job must be the reason that you got the occupational disease or added additional likelihood of exposure. By proving all three of these things, the employee is entitled to receive medical and disability benefits for their injuries.

The first thing that you must prove is that bilateral carpal tunnel syndrome is a disease that must be one of which others in your trade or occupation has a likely chance of catching. North Carolina law has clearly defined an occupational disease. A disease is linked to the profession when there is a greater risk of catching the disease because of the type of work being done. In your case, you did a lot of work that placed a great deal of pressure on your hands. As a tire builder, you were required to do things that included gripping, cutting, and pressing tire components with both of your hands. For example, you had to grip shears in your right hand and press them into the palm of your hand while cutting tire pieces. You had been doing this type of work for twenty-four years. Based on your work with Badtreads, you were placed at a greater risk of getting bilateral carpal tunnel syndrome. Therefore, bilateral carpal tunnel syndrome was a likely result of your employment and is a disease that others in your line of work may also develop.

The second thing that you must prove is that bilateral carpal tunnel syndrome is not an ordinary disease that others outside of your job can catch equally. This means that even individuals who are not tire builders have an equal chance of getting bilateral carpal tunnel syndrome from their employment. Your assignments at work included not only building tires, but also pushing heavy equipment with the palms of your hands. The heavy equipment weighed about 1,000 pounds. This type of work was continuous, as it went on during your eight-hour shifts at a rate of twenty times per shift. Doctors are the best source for determining the disease's potential harm to the general public. Doctors would agree that bilateral carpal tunnel syndrome is not a common disease such as the flu. For these reasons, you have bilateral carpal tunnel syndrome, a disease that is uncommon to the general public.

The third thing that you must prove is that your employment is the reason that you have the occupational disease. In your case, this is the best explanation for your bilateral carpal tunnel syndrome. There were several reasons that your employment led to your current condition: (1) the amount of work your were doing with your hands in the eight- and twelve-hour shifts; (2) the length of time that you were employed at Badtreads doing the work; and (3) the time period when you first noticed problems with your hands. Additionally, you had no other employment after you had been out of work with Badtreads. So, there are no outside factors for your bilateral carpal tunnel syndrome. Therefore, your employment at Badtreads is the reason that you have bilateral carpal tunnel syndrome.

Based upon your injuries, you are entitled to receive medical and disability benefits for your bilateral carpal tunnel syndrome.

In summary, these conclusions are opinions as to your possibility of receiving compensation for your injuries from Badtreads. It is likely that you will have a chance to receive compensation and medical benefits from Badtreads for your bilateral carpal tunnel syndrome, so you should pursue action against Badtreads. You should be able to receive benefits for three reasons. First, bilateral carpal tunnel syndrome is an occupational disease that others in your line of work may obtain. Second, bilateral carpal tunnel syndrome is not an ordinary disease that others outside of your line of work can catch equally. Third, your employment at Badtreads led to your bilateral carpal syndrome. But the final decision is yours on whether you would like to pursue action against them for your injuries.

I would like to thank you for your patience through this process. If you would like to retain our firm as your legal representative, please contact the office at (919) 897-3556. Please contact us if you have any questions about this letter, or any other issues about your case.

Sincerely,
Jamar Creech

Example H-2

N.C. Central Law Firm
1512 S. Alston Ave.
Durham, North Carolina 27707
919-929-3905

Mrs. Beatrice Potter
13-B Imperial Garden Apartments
555 Hood Dr.
Shatley Springs, NC 28911

Re: Opinion Letter About Your Case

Dear Mrs. Potter:

We are writing this letter to provide you with more information concerning the injuries you sustained during your time as a tenant at the Imperial Gardens Apartment Complex that you discussed with us. Please take the time to review the letter and the information included therein. It is our hope that after reading this letter, you will have an understanding of how the law operates with respect to your situation, and what options are available to you as a plaintiff.

POTENTIAL CLAIMS

There are three claims that are potentially available to you as the plaintiff in your individual capacity: intentional infliction of emotional distress, negligence, and negligent infliction of emotional distress. You may also potentially bring a wrongful death claim for Peter's death in your capacity as administratrix of Peter's estate. However, there are certain elements of each claim that we must prove in order for you to be successful and obtain any damages for your injuries. We will break down each element for you and explain how we intend to satisfy each element so that your claim will be successful.

Intentional Infliction of Emotional Distress

For intentional infliction of emotional distress, we must prove that the party you are suing acted intentionally or recklessly, that their behavior went beyond what anyone in decent society would be expected to tolerate, and that their behavior caused you severe emotional distress.

In the case of the McClouds, the first element would be satisfied because their behavior and inaction once confronted with numerous instances of criminal activity in the complex would be considered reckless. A person's behavior is considered reckless when they show a disregard for the health and safety of others. The McClouds demonstrated reckless behavior when they failed to evict known drug dealers and criminals after being warned by the housing inspector of Shatley Springs to do so. They failed to take action after they received numerous police reports of criminal activity in and around the complex. Furthermore, when they were approached by Mr. Doyle and the Shatley Springs housing inspector, on both occasions they indicated their desire that the residents of the complex would eventually kill each other. Such behavior showed a disregard for the health and safety of you and your grandson as tenants of Imperial Gardens.

With respect to the second element, no one in decent society would expect anyone, especially a tenant in an apartment complex, to tolerate being forced to continue living around known criminals and drug dealers who commit acts of violence in the living area on a regular basis. The term "decent society" simply refers to the average citizen in a community with certain morals and expectations of decency. However, the McClouds may argue that their behavior in failing to evict known criminals did not exceed the bounds of what would be tolerated by decent society. Fortunately, we feel that such an argument is not supported by the information you gave us.

For purposes of proving severe emotional distress, we must show some mental harm you suffered that was diagnosed by a physician. Because the landlords failed to evict these criminals and to take action to keep you and the other tenants safe, you suffered severe emotional distress through witnessing the death of your grandson by gunfire. We have information concerning your hospitalization for your heart attack, depression, and post-traumatic stress disorder. This is more than enough to show that you suffered severe emotional distress, and that your distress was connected to the failure of the landlords to keep the premises safe.

Negligence

In North Carolina, a party must prove four elements to be successful on a claim of negligence: duty, breach, causation, and damages. The concept of duty simply means that as landlords, the McClouds had certain obligations to you as a tenant to keep the premises safe and in good condition. Breach means that they failed to satisfy these obligations. Causation determines that their failure to satisfy those obligations to you was the legal cause of the harm that you suffered. Finally, damages are simply the losses you suffered as a result of your injury. Not only would we have to prove the elements of negligence with respect to your injuries, but we would also have to prove them with respect to Peter's death to support your claim for wrongful death as administratrix of his estate.

As your landlords, the McClouds had a duty to keep the premises safe and in good condition. Generally, with respect to having a duty to protect tenants from criminal activity, a landlord must have notice of criminal activity on or around the premises. From what you told us, there was more than enough evidence given to the McClouds to make them aware of the criminal activity that was taking place in the complex.

First, the McClouds received the letter that was written to them by you, Mr. Doyle, and several other residents which addressed gunfire that resulted in damage to Mr. Doyle's car. The McClouds also had police reports detailing incidents on and around the premises such as fistfights, beatings, and gunfire. In addition, the housing inspector for Shatley Springs warned the McClouds that they needed to evict known criminals and drug dealers from the complex. Finally, CP&L issued a directive requiring any employee of the company to be accompanied by law enforcement whenever they entered the apartment complex. This was in response to an incident where a CP&L employee was severely beaten while trying to disconnect electricity in an apartment in Imperial Gardens. All of these reported incidents and warnings show that the McClouds had actual notice of criminal activity in the complex, and that it was reasonably foreseeable that if they failed to take action, such activity would continue to occur. Therefore they owed you and your grandson a duty to keep the premises safe.

The second element, breach, is satisfied because the McClouds did not take action to remedy the situation. They did not hire security guards for the complex until AFTER your grandson was killed. Prior to the incident involving your grandson, when the McClouds were given information about dangerous activity, they failed to respond, even going so far as to indicate that they hoped the residents would ultimately kill each other off over a period of time.

The third element, causation, is satisfied as well. In order to satisfy this element, we must show that it was reasonably foreseeable that the landlords' breach of the duty they owed would result in an injury. Because you were not directly injured, but only suffered injury because of your relationship to Peter, the court would look at certain factors to determine if it was reasonably foreseeable to the landlords that their behavior would cause you to suffer harm as well as Peter. The court would look at your proximity (closeness in space and time) to the negligent acts of the McClouds, your relationship to the person directly injured, and finally, whether you personally saw the negligent act of the McClouds.

As you informed us on your initial visit, you were standing with Peter when the gunshots were fired that resulted in his death. You had been a resident of the complex for years, and so you had firsthand knowledge of the fact that the McClouds were negligent in keeping the premises safe for the residents. Also, you had a close relationship with the person injured, Peter, as his grandmother and his primary caretaker. In short, we would be able to prove that it was foreseeable to the McClouds that their negligent behavior would cause you to suffer harm based on your relationship with Peter.

Finally, we must show that you suffered damages as a result of the landlord's negligence. As mentioned previously, you have evidence of your hospitalization for the heart attack you suffered, as well as the diagnoses of depression and post-traumatic stress disorder. This information is sufficient to show that you suffered damages as a result of your landlords' negligence.

Negligent Infliction of Emotional Distress

On your claim of negligent infliction of emotional distress, we must show that the defendant (the McClouds and the Complex) was negligent, that it was foreseeable to the defendant that his negligence would cause you severe emotional distress, and that the conduct, in fact, caused you severe emotional distress.

We would be able to satisfy all of the elements for this claim. Based on the information you provided us, we will be able to prove that the McClouds were negligent, thus satisfying the first element. As mentioned previously in the discussion of the negligence claim, as Peter's grandmother, it is understandable and foreseeable that witnessing any injury to him would cause you to suffer severe emotional distress. Finally, because of the depression and post-traumatic stress disorder that you suffered, you would be able to satisfy the element of severe emotional distress.

Wrongful Death

In your position as administratrix of Peter's estate, you would be able to bring a wrongful death action on his behalf. In order to be successful on a claim of wrongful death, a party must prove that the decedent's death was due to the wrongful act or negligence of another. In your case, we would prove that Peter's death was a result of the negligence of the McClouds. Once again, we would use the elements that we used to satisfy your negligence claim. With respect to Peter, all of the elements would be satisfied. The landlords owed him a duty of care. They breached it by not providing protection or evicting criminals. Their failure to take proper action was the legal cause of Peter's death, and damages in the form of medical and funeral expenses were incurred.

PARTIES LIABLE

Based on the facts you presented to us, it appears that the parties you would bring suit against are Patrick and Duncan McCloud and Imperial Gardens Apartment Complex. Patrick and Duncan would each be liable, because as your landlords, they had certain obligations to you as a tenant during your time at Imperial Gardens. The Complex would be brought in as a party, because it is a partnership under North Carolina law. With this being the case, the partnership as a whole is responsible for the actions of the partners if they cause injury to anyone. If we are successful in proving the elements of each claim you wish to bring, these are the parties who would be required to compensate you for your injuries and your loss.

DAMAGES

If you decide to bring a claim against the McClouds and the Imperial Gardens Apartment Complex, you would be entitled to receive compensatory and punitive damages. Compensatory damages are damages that arise from expenses in relation to an injury. This includes past and future medical expenses, damages allotted for pain and suffering, funeral expenses, loss of earnings, etc.

As compensation for your injuries, we would be able to recover the value of your medical expenses, which would include your hospitalization and any prescriptions that you were given as a result of that hospitalization. In addition, we would be able to receive compensation for any future doctor visits that are related to the injuries you suffered in this particular incident. This would include more prescriptions for medication, visits with your psychiatrist, and any potential surgeries or other medical procedures that would have to be done with respect to your heart attack.

As compensation under a wrongful death claim, you would receive the value of Peter's medical expenses when he was taken to the hospital after the shooting. You would also receive compensation for reasonable funeral expenses from Peter's burial. Also, because Peter was still alive when he was taken to the hospital, you could potentially receive compensation for his pain and suffering during that time.

Punitive damages are awarded when the defendant's behavior is considered malicious or deliberate in nature. In essence, such damages are used to send a message to the defendants that their behavior was wrong and to deter them from engaging in such conduct in the future. The amount of punitive damages you may be awarded will be based on the amount of compensatory damages that you receive. In North Carolina, a plaintiff will either receive punitive damages in an amount that is three times the amount they received in compensatory damages, or they may receive $250,000.00. Generally the court will award the larger amount.

The McClouds' behavior in refusing to evict known criminals and in indicating a desire to have the residents kill each other shows malice and is deliberate in nature. Therefore, it is likely that you will be able to recover punitive damages in addition to recovering compensatory damages.

STATUTES OF LIMITATION

In North Carolina, each claim that is brought must be brought within a certain time period that is determined by statute. If the claim is not filed within a certain time period, an individual will find that the claim is completely barred and may not be brought.

With respect to a claim for intentional infliction of emotional distress, the time period in which we must bring suit is ten years after the injuries you suffered. This means that you must bring an action against the McClouds and Imperial Gardens by December 2017; otherwise, your claim will be barred.

In regard to claims for negligence and negligent infliction of emotional distress, we must bring these claims within three years after the last negligent act of the McClouds and Imperial Gardens. A lawsuit for the wrongful death of Peter must be brought within two years after his death.

COURSE OF ACTION

At this point, we must sit down with you to decide on a course of action. We would suggest attempting to settle with the McClouds and Imperial Gardens Apartment Complex. To this end, once you have read this letter, please call us so that we may proceed to the next step. We understand that you have been through a great deal of trauma, and we wish to assist you in seeking justice for yourself, as well as Peter.

Sincerely,
Student

APPENDIX I

✝

DEMAND LETTER/SETTLEMENT BROCHURE

Law Firm
1338 Main Street
Springfield, NC 28901

25 April 2008

David Jones, Claims Adjuster
Freedom Insurance
PO Box 2345
Charlotte, NC 20220

RE: John Doe, Workers' Compensation Claim No. 567890ASDF

Dear Mr. Jones:

As you know from our earlier conversations, my client, John Doe, is seeking to recover workers' compensation damages for injuries sustained while he was working. Mr. Doe sustained injuries to his arm, clavicle, and leg. He has spent a large sum of money on medical attention. Accordingly, Mr. Doe has authorized me to accept $140,000.00 to settle this case.

Mr. Doe is thirty-seven years old. He received his high school diploma from Jackson High School in Broome, N.C. After high school, he worked as a groundskeeper at Broome County Park for three years. He has no other formal training. In 1991, Mr. Doe began working as a general laborer with 123 Construction. His position involved working with the roofers and the brick masons. [Exhibit A] Mr. Doe tossed heavy bricks to laborers on scaffolding and brought materials to the roof for the roofers.

On 5 January 2006, while taking roofing materials to the roof via scaffolding and a pulley contraption, Mr. Doe fell 3 stories to the ground below. He suffered a broken right wrist, elbow, and clavicle. He also fractured his left leg and sustained several broken toes. [Exhibit B] His coworkers all saw the fall and ran to alert the supervisor. The supervisor, Randy Parker, called for emergency help. But as Mr. Doe was being loaded into the ambulance, Randy told Mr. Doe not to report the fall under workers' compensation. Randy assured Mr. Doe that his health insurance through the construction company, ABC Health, would pay for all medical bills.

Mr. Doe filed all of his medical claims under ABC Health, which paid for everything except for his $1,000.00 deductible and applicable co-pays. After initial surgeries, Dr. Jane Sampson informed Mr. Doe that he needed an additional surgery to save his right arm, which had not healed properly. After getting paperwork from Dr. Sampson's office, ABC Health realized that the injury came from a work accident and refused to pay for any further surgery, stating that 123 Construction's workers' compensation insurance through Freedom Insurance should be liable for the surgery charges. [Exhibit C]

At that time, Mr. Doe was afraid that he would lose his arm and finally reported the injury as a workers' compensation claim to 123 Construction on 12 December 2007. Since ABC Health had already paid for much of Mr. Doe's medical expenses, 123 Construction asked Freedom Insurance to refuse to pay and see if ABC Health would pay for the needed surgery. Mr. Doe has paid or owes $11,262.97 in medical treatment [Exhibit D] and is entitled to $84,766.59 in disability based on the compensation rate of his average weekly wage pursuant to N.C. Gen. Stat. § 97-31 (2010). [Exhibit E] He is willing to settle the entire claim, which includes future medical treatment for $140,000.00. This demand is open for thirty days after the date of this letter. Please call me to discuss settlement. I look forward to speaking with you.

Sincerely,
Settlement Attorney

Exhibit A: Job Description
123 Construction
1685 State Street
Springfield, NC 28911

Wanted: GENERAL LABORER

Job Description: Perform various tasks involved with building structures, including homes and commercial buildings. Must be able to lift at least 75 lbs. Required to work on roofs as well as on the ground. Some scaffolding work required, but only 25% of the time. Will serve as an assistant to certified brick masons and roofers.

Education: High school diploma required.

MUST BE ABLE TO PASS PHYSICAL EXAM

** Position subject to random drug testing

Exhibit B: Doctor's Notes

Jane Sampson, MD
200 Discovery Avenue
Springfield, NC 28911
February 11, 2008

Mr. John Doe
1500 James Street
Springfield, NC 28912

Dear John:

I know that you are trying to figure out how to pay for the additional surgery, but we cannot wait too much longer. If you arm continues to heal improperly, the necessary amount of blood will not circulate to it and we will have to amputate it sometime down the road. As you have asked me to do, I have attached a summary of your medical records to this letter for you to take to an attorney. Let's work together to get the medical care that you need and deserve. Please let me know if I can be of any further service.

Sincerely,

Jane Sampson

Jane Sampson, MD

8/31/2005   Checked out sprained knee after fall while playing football with friends. Referred for X-ray.

9/1/2005   X-ray is normal. Prescribed muscle relaxer and pain meds.

3/13/2006   John fell 3 stories while at work. Suffered broken right wrist (fractured in 2 places), broken right elbow (reset at SC Hosp.), broken right clavicle (closer to shoulder than neck). Left leg broken in two places below femur. Three broken toes (one on right foot, two on left foot). Will continue with meds prescribed at hospital. We will need to take additional X-rays after 1.5 months. Cast and crutches okay. Out of work for 1 month.

4/15/2006   Removed left leg cast. He is able to walk on it with a brace. All toes are untaped and moveable. His right arm is still giving him pain. Upped pain meds. Muscle relaxers not helping. Out of work for 1 month.

4/20/2006   Removed arm cast. He is not able to move it as he should be able to do. Keep cast off and fitted him with soft brace. Maybe using it a little at a time will help.

4/27/2006   More pain with right arm. Leg and toes are fine. Can remove leg brace. Need additional X-rays and MRI on right arm.

4/28/2006   MRI shows that the tendons in right elbow have snapped and blood loss is increasing due to the twisting of the ligaments at elbow. Needs new surgery asap. Will see if insurance co will authorize so we can schedule surgery. Remain out of work until after surgery.

6/1/2006   Health insurance company that has been paying all bills will not authorize additional surgery because they just learned that this is a work-related injury.

7/1/2006   Spoke with John, he does not want to file a workers' comp case because supervisor told him not to. Still cannot get authorization for arm surgery.

9/12/2006   Spoke with John, he does not want to file a workers' comp case because supervisor told him not to. Still cannot get authorization for arm surgery. John experiencing more pain and requests pain meds. Will prescribe, but only for 2 more months. He needs surgery, not meds.

11/18/2006   Refilled meds.

2/28/2007   Right arm getting worse. Went through compression exercises.

4/9/2007   MRI ordered.

7/1/2007   Check-up. Respondent arm still getting worse.

10/14/2007   Check-up. Same findings. Patient feeling increased pain.

11/30/2007   MRI shows worsening of the arm. We need to discuss the probability of amputation.

12/12/2007   Patient called. Finally reported to workers' comp.

1/2/2008   Workers' comp ins co denying claim. Patient still needs the arm surgery. The arm looks swollen and discolored. John still cannot return to work until he has this surgery. At this point, John has been out of work for several months. He believes that his supervisor will tell the WC ins to pay for the surgery if he can come back to work soon afterwards.

2/1/2008   John has been on disability, but he is not receiving the money he thinks he should be getting. Now, he cannot afford the pain meds. Have not heard from client except message about denied claim.

1/31/2008   Balance in this office as of this date: $7,632.97

Disability ratings: Right wrist: 35%

Right elbow: 55%

Right clavicle: 10%

Left leg: 25%

Three broken toes: 5%, 7% 10%

Exhibit C: Letter from Health Insurance Company

ABC Health

2809 MLK Boulevard, Suite 900

Savannah, GA 33333

May 1, 2006

Mr. John Doe

1500 James Street

Springfield, NC 28912

Dear Mr. Doe:

We have been informed that your injury on January 5, 2006, stemmed from a work-related incident. Because of this, your employer's workers' compensation insurance company should be paying for your medical expenses. We will continue to deny authorization for any medical expenses related to any work-related incident. We are also seeking compensation for the monies we have paid on your behalf before we realized the context of this injury. You may call our toll-free line for further information.

Sincerely,

Tiffany Walkington

Tiffany Walkington, Claims Representative

Exhibit D: Hospital Bill

Springfield County Hospital
100 Discovery Avenue
Springfield, NC 28911

January 21, 2008

Mr. John Doe
1500 James Street
Springfield, NC 28912

Dear Mr. Doe:

We have tried to contact you several times regarding the balances due on your account. Please refer to the following chart to see the charges and payments that have been made on this account within the last two years. We look forward to receiving your payment immediately.

Date	Service Rendered	Cost	Amount paid by you	Amount paid by ins. co	Amount Due
3/5/06	EMERGENCY ROOM VISIT	$545.00	$145.00	$275.00	$125.00
3/5/06	X-RAY	$400.00	$0	$350.00	$50.00
3/7/06	EMERGENCY ROOM VISIT	$545.00	$50.00	$495.00	$0
3/11/06	X-RAY	$400.00	$0	$350.00	$50.00
3/11/06	ROOM	$2,000.00	$0	$1,000.00	$1,000.00
3/11/06	MEDS	$255.00	$55.00	$100.00	$100.00

3/12/06	ROOM	$2,000.00	$0	$2000.00	$0
3/12/06	MEDS	$255.00	$0	$100.00	$155.00
3/12/06	ORTHOPAEDIC MATERIALS (CAST, CRUTCHES, ETC.)	$1,500.00	$0	$1,300.00	$200.00
4/28/06	X-RAY AND MRI	$1,200.00	$200.00	$500.00	$500.00
11/1/07	MRI	$1,000.00	$0	$0	$1,000.00
TOTAL		$10,100.00	$450.00	$6,470.00	$3,180.00

Exhibit E: Pay stubs

123 Construction

Doe, John
1500 James Street
Springfield, N.C. 28912

Pay stub: General Laborer $12/hour

WEEK	MONDAY	TUESDAY	WEDNESDAY	THURSDAY	FRIDAY	SATURDAY	SUNDAY	PAY
FEB 1	7.0	7.0	7.0	7.0	7.0	7.0		504
FEB 2	7.0	7.0	7.0	7.0	7.0	7.0		504
FEB 3	7.0	7.0	7.0	7.0	7.0	7.0		504
FEB 4	7.0	7.0	7.0	7.0	7.0	7.0		504

WEEK	MONDAY	TUESDAY	WEDNESDAY	THURSDAY	FRIDAY	SATURDAY	SUNDAY	PAY
MAR 1	7.0	7.0	7.0	7.0	7.0	7.0		504
MAR 2	7.0	7.0	7.0	7.0	7.0	7.0		504
MAR 3	7.0	7.0	7.0	7.0	7.0	7.0		504
MAR 4	7.0	7.0	7.0	7.0	7.0	7.0		504

WEEK	MONDAY	TUESDAY	WEDNESDAY	THURSDAY	FRIDAY	SATURDAY	SUNDAY	PAY
APR 1	7.0	7.0	7.0	7.0	7.0	7.0		504
APR 2	7.0	7.0	7.0	7.0	7.0	7.0		504
APR 3	7.0	7.0	7.0	7.0	7.0	7.0		504
APR 4	7.0	7.0	7.0	7.0	7.0	7.0		504

APPENDIX J
✝
CITATIONS

Using *A Uniform System of Citation* (18th ed.), write or choose the correct citation for each of the following. Note that citations are in legal memoranda or documents being submitted to state courts unless otherwise indicated. Additionally, **pay particular attention to punctuation, abbreviation, and spacing.**

Exercise J-1

You wish to cite to the case of Brian Kennedy versus Wachovia Mortgage Corporation. The case was decided by the California Court of Appeals on December 4, 2006 and is found in volume 76 of the West's California Reporter, Second Series at page 1906.

Kennedy v. Wachovia Mortgage Corp., **76 Cal. Rptr. 2d 1906 (Cal. Ct. App. 2006).**

R.10.2.1(g)	**Generally omit given names or initials of individuals.**
R.10.3.2	**A citation to a reporter consists of a volume designation, the abbreviated name of the reporter, and the page on which the case report begins.**
R.10.4(b)	**Omit the jurisdiction (but not the court abbreviation) if it is unambiguously conveyed by the reporter title unless the decision is rendered by the** highest **court in the state.**

T.1	**California Court of Appeal.**
B5.1–B5.1.1.4	**Bluepages tips/examples for case citations.**
B.5.1.1 &	**Italicize or underline the entire case name up to, but not including, the comma that follows.**
B5.1.3(iii)	**Numerals and ordinals are treated as single capitals.**
T.6	**Abbreviate case names (corporation).**

2. You wish to cite to California Code of Regulations. The provision you are referencing is in Title 6 and Section 1299 and it was published in 2009.

Cal. Code Regs. tit. 6, § 1299 (2009).

T.1	**Administrative compilation.**

3. You want to reference the previously cited case from Footnote one, pages 1909 and 1912.

Kennedy, **76 Cal. Rptr. 2d at 1909, 1912. or**
76 Cal. Rptr. 2d at 1909, 1912.

R. 10.9	**Short citation forms.**
R.10.9(a)(i)	**When using only one party name in a short form citation, avoid using the name of a geographical or governmental unit or other common litigant.**

4. You wish to cite to the case of the Illinois Commissioner of Banks versus Branch Banking and Trust. This case was decided by the Illinois Supreme Court on January 15, 2008, and is found in volume 92 of the North Eastern Reporter, Second Series, at page 1908.

Ill. Comm'r of Banks v. Branch Banking & Trust, 92 N.E.2d 1908 (Ill. 2008).

T.1	Illinois Supreme Court.
T.6	Case Names.
T.10	Geographic names.
R. 10.2.2	Abbreviate "and."
R. 10.4(b)	Identify the state.

5. You wish to reference the previously cited case from Footnote four Id.

R.10.9   **Examples of short forms for cases.**

6.   You wish to cite to the Fourteenth Amendment to the United States Constitution, section five.

U.S. Const. amend. XIV, § 5.

R.11   **Cite to federal Constitution.**

7. You wish to cite the case of Jimmie Bugg Middleton versus Ivy Bank Incorporated. The case was decided by the United States Supreme Court on January 29, 1913, and is found in volume 108 of the Supreme Court Reporter at page 425, volume 616, of the United States Reports at page 765, and volume 63 of the United States Supreme Court Reports, Lawyers' Edition, at page 199.

  Middleton v. Ivy Bank, Inc., **616 U.S. 765 (1913).**

T.6	**Abbreviations for case names.**
R.10	**Illustration of a U.S. Supreme Court case.**
T.1	**"Federal"—order of preference for Supreme Court reporters.**

8. You wish to cite to Title 28 of the United States Code, section 1910. The date of the latest edition is 2009.

28	**U.S.C. § 1910 (2009).**
R.3	Example of United States code.
R.12.3.1	

9. You wish to cite to case of Henry Arthur Callis versus Polemark Lenders of America, Incorporated. The case was decided on January 5, 2001, by the Fifth Circuit Court of Appeals. The case can be found in volume 420 of the Federal Reporter, second edition, and begins on page 1906. You want to cite to pages 1906 through 1911.

Callis v. Polemark Lenders of Am., Inc., 420 F.2d 1960, 1906-11 (5th Cir. 2001).

T.6	**Abbreviations for case names.**
T.1	**Fifth Circuit Court of Appeals.**
R.3.2	**Multiple pages.**
T.7	**Court names.**
R.10.2.1(f)	**Include designations of national or larger geographical areas.**
R.10.2.2	**Always abbreviate any word listed in T.6.**

10. You wish to cite to the California Property statutes that define foreclosure. The statute is located in the West Annotated codes in the Civil subject area. The statute is located in section 1467 and was last published in 2009.

Cal. Civ. Code § 14-67 (West 2009).
T.1   **California statutory compilations.**

11. You wish to cite the Federal Rules of Civil Procedure, Rule 18. The rule has not been amended since 2005, but was last published in 2009.

Fed. R. Civ. P. 18.
R.12.8.3   **Rules of Civil Procedure.**

Exercise J-2

1. You are preparing a brief to submit to the North Carolina Court of Appeals, and you wish to cite to the case of The State of North Carolina versus Rick Smalls, Ernest Eckert, Catawba County, and the Sheriff of Catawba County, Defendants. The case was argued before the North Carolina Supreme Court on August 5, 2002, and decided on January 13, 2003, and is found in Volume 355 of the North Carolina Reporter beginning on page 230, and Volume 558 of the Southeastern Reporter, second series, beginning on page 464. The local rules of the North Carolina Court of Appeals require a parallel cite to the official state reporter, followed by a parallel cite to the regional reporter.

State v. Smalls**, 355 N.C. 230, 558 S.E.2d 464 (2003).**

R.10.2.1(f)	**Omit "State of," except when citing decisions of the courts of that state, in which case only "State" should be retained.**
R.10.2.1(a)	**Omit all parties, other than the first listed on each side.**
R.10.3.2 A	**Citation to a reporter consists of a volume designation, the abbreviated name of the reporter, and the page on which the case report begins.**
R.10.3.1(a)	**If local rules for citation in documents submitted to state courts differ from BB rules, follow the local rules.**
R.10.4(b)	**When a decision is rendered by the highest court in the jurisdiction and the name of the reporter is the same as the**

name of that jurisdiction, neither the name of the court nor the name of the state need be given.

T.1	**North Carolina.**
B5.1-B5.1.1.4	**Bluepages tips/examples for case citations.**
B.13	**Case names are italicized or underscored.**
R.6.1(a)	**In general, close up adjacent single capitals; individual numbrs, including numerals and ordinals, are treated as single capitals.**

2. a. You wish to cite to page 10 of the case, The United States on behalf of Exxon Mobil Corporation versus Allpath Service, Incorporated, et al., Maria Del Rosario Ortega, et al. The case was argued on March 1, 2005, and decided by the United States District Court in the Southern District of New York on October 3, 2005. You found the case, which is unreported, on the Westlaw database. The database identifier is 2005 WL 282775 and the docket number is No. 05-9752.

United States ex rel. Exxon Mobil Corp. v. Allpath Serv., Inc., No. 05-9752, 2005 WL 282775, at *10 (S.D.N.Y. Oct. 3, 2005).

R.18.1.1	**When a case is unreported but available on a widely used electronic database, it may be cited to that database; provide the case name, docket number, database identifier, court name, and full date of the most recent major disposition of the case. Screen or page numbers should be preceded by an asterisk.**
R.10.2.1(b)	**Abbreviate "on behalf of" to "ex rel." When adversary parties are named, omit all procedural phrases except "exrel."**
R.10.2.2	**Abbreviate states, countries, and other geographical units, unless the geographical unit is the entire name of the party. This includes "United States."**
T.6	**Abbreviations of case names.**
R.6.1	**Insert a space adjacent to any abbreviation containing two or more letters.**

b. After several intervening citations you wish to refer to page 4 of the case in 2a.
Exxon Mobil Corp., **2005 WL 282775, at *4.**

**Please note that there are other acceptable shortened case names, i.e., Allpath Serv.
Inc., United States ex rel. Exxon.**

| R.18.7 | Short forms for electronic databases. |

3. You wish to cite to the case of In the Matter of Maryland Casualty Company, Inc.
The case was decided by the United States Court of Appeals for the Ninth Circuit on
December 16, 1991, but you cannot find the official reporter. Instead, you have found
the case at paragraph 5068 in the 1991–1992 Transfer Binder of the Products Liability
Reports (a loose-leaf service), which is published by Commerce Clearing House. The date
of the volume is 1992.

In re Md. Cas. Co., **[1991–1992 Transfer Binder] Prod. Liab. Rep. (CCH) ¶ 5068
(9th Cir. Dec. 16, 1991).**

R.10.2.1(b)	**Omit all procedural phrases except the first.**
R.10.2.1(h)	**Omit "Inc." if the name also contains a word such as**
	Company, clearly indicating that the party is a business firm.
10.2.2/T.6	**Abbreviations of case names.**
T.10	**Table of Geographical Terms.**
R.19.1	**Citation to a service.**
T.15	**Table of services.**
T.1(federal)	**Table of jurisdictions.**
R.6.1(a)	**Spacing.**
R.6.2(c).	**¶ symbols.**
R.19.1(d)	**Date.**

4.a.You have found Title 35, Criminal Law and Procedure, Article 42, Offenses Against
the Person,

Chapter 1, Homicide, of the Burns Indiana Statutes Annotated. You are specifically
interested in section
35-42-1-6(1). No year appears on the spine of the volume; the year 1997 appears on
the title page; the year
1998 is the copyright date of the volume.

Ind. Code Ann. § 35-42-1-6(1)   (LexisNexis 1997).

R.3.3   **Sections and paragraphs.**

R.6.2(c)   **Use symbols for sections and paragraphs and separate from numeral with a space.**

R.12   **General rules for statutory citations.**

T.1   **Rules for statutory citations by jurisdiction.**

R.12.3.2   **Provide parenthetically the year that appears on the spine of the volume, the year that appears on the title page, or the latest copyright year—in that order of preference.**

B. You wish to cite to Section 35-42-1-6(2) and there are no intervening citations.
Id. § 35-42-1-6(2). or § 35-42-1-6(2).

B5   **The "i" in "id." is only capitalized when it begins a citation sentence. The underline always runs under the period.**

R.12.9   **Examples of short forms for statutes.**

R.3.3   **Do not use "at" before a section or paragraph symbol.**

5. You wish to cite to the Thirteenth Amendment to the United States Constitution.
U.S. Const. amend. XIII. R.11

Exercise J-3

1. You wish to cite to a law review note written and signed by Henry Callis, Charles Chapman, and George Kelly, entitled "The Race is on for the Gold," which appeared at page 7 in volume 201 of the National Journal for the Evolution of College Life (a consecutively paginated journal), published in 2006. You wish to focus the reader's attention to pages 55 and 56 of the article.

2. After several intervening citations, you want to reference the article from Question 1, focusing on page 15.

3. You heard a very moving speech by the first African-American Secretary of the Department of Energy. You want to cite the speech in your law review article. The Speaker is Hazel O'Leary. She was speaking at Howard University's commencement on May 1, 2001. Her topic was "It's All Dick's Fault."

4. You have spoken with a professor who is working on an article that will be perfect for your supervising attorney's case. Unfortunately, the article is still a working paper, No.

2. The year you have accessed the document is 2007. You have decided to cite it in your brief. Your professor's name is Barack W. Clinton. He will publish it in the International and Comparative Law Quarterly. The article will be called "Between I Have a Dream and I Have a Plan." The abstract of the article is available at http://www.barackhillary.com. You want to focus attention on pages 10–12.

5. You wish to cite to page 15 of the article in Question 4, and there are no intervening citations.

6. You ran across Dr. Steve Dunk's dissertation. You want to cite this unpublished work in a brief to the Court. The title of the dissertation is "First of All, Servants of All, We Shall Transcend." While this was an enlightening work, it was never published. The dissertation was completed on April 10, 2000, and kept on file at Anderson Library at St. Augustine's College, when Dr. Dunk obtained his PhD.

7. You wish to cite to section 34 of the Restatement of Torts which was published on May 10, 2006.

ANSWERS TO J-3

1. Henry Callis, Charles Chapman, & George Kelly, The Race is on for the Gold, 201 Nat'l J. for the Evolution of C. Life, 7 55-56 (2006).

—Or—

Henry Callis et al., The Race is on for the Gold, 201 Nat'l J. for the Evolution of C. Life, 7 55-56 (2006).

R.16.1(15.1)	Give the full name of the author(s), followed by a comma.
16.2	Cite the full periodical title as it appears on the title page, but capitalize according to R.8.
R.8	Capitalization.
R.16.3	Cite works in consecutively paginated periodicals by author(s), title of work, volume number, periodical name, first page of the work, page(s) on which specific material appears.
R.3.2	Properly listing pages and pin cites.
T.13	Proper abbreviation for the periodical.

2. Callis, supra at 15.

R. 4.2	
R. 16.7	
B9.2	Short-form citation.

3. Hazel O'Leary, Sec'y Dep't of Energy, Keynote Address at Howard University Commencement: It's All Dick's Fault (May 1, 2001).

R. 17.1.5   The speaker's title and institutional affiliation should be abbreviated according to T.6 & T.10.

4. Barack W. Clinton, "Between I Have a Dream and I Have a Plan" 10–12 (Int'l & Comp. L.Q., Working Paper No. 2–1999), available at http://www.barackhillary. com.

R.17.3
T.2
5.Id. at 15
R.41
6. Steve Dunk "First Of All, Servants Of All, We Shall Transcend All" (April 10, 2000) (unpublished PhD. dissertation, St. Augustine's College) (on file with Anderson Library, St. Augustine's College).

R.17.1
R.17.1.1
R. 17.1.2

APPENDIX K

⸸

CONCLUDING EXERCISE

Often law students are presented with a fact pattern and a set of cases. They are then asked to write an objective memorandum. This exercise is very similar to the way summer associates and new attorneys assist the other attorneys at the firm. When you are given the cases that you must use, this is called a "closed world" assignment. When you are free to research and locate your own cases, this is an "open world" assignment.

Remember to always read the prompt carefully. Answer the questions raised by the facts and the prompt. If there is a potential issue raised by the facts, but omitted from the prompt, do not address it.

Read the following fact pattern and cases. Then work through the exercises.

MEMORANDUM

To: Summer Associate
From: Joseph P. Johnson, Senior Associate
Date: October 31, 2008
Re: Potential Predatory Lending Case

We represent Dee Black. She is the sole beneficiary of her mother's estate. Dee's mother, Cee, passed away in 2007. Cee had a doctorate in Women's Studies. She had been a professor at a local university for many years before she retired in 2003. Cee and her late husband purchased one home many years ago. At the time of her death, the home was co-owned by Cee and her special friend, Eddi. They owned the property jointly, as joint tenants in common. Cee left her one-half interest in the property to her daughter, Dee. Eddi still lives in the property. The property is a single family residence located in Monroe, North Carolina. The home is valued at $60,000.00.

Eddi has advised Dee that Dee needs to start paying half of the monthly mortgage payment, because Eddi cannot afford to pay it by herself. Eddi says that the mortgage balance is $74,000.00, and the monthly payment is $1,500.00,, not including the taxes and insurance, which are paid separately.

Dee was shocked to discover that Eddi owned half of the home and she was even more shocked to learn that the home was encumbered by a $74,000.00 mortgage. This home was built by Dee's father in the early 1920s. Dee grew up in that home and always planned to retire there. Dee thought that the home was free and clear of any loans.

After contacting the mortgage company, Fast Cash Mortgage Company, Dee discovered the following:

On May 1, 2006, Cee granted Eddi a one-half interest in the property. This was done to allow Eddi to take out a loan on the property. At the time, the property was encumbered by a mortgage with a $15,000.00 balance and a monthly payment of $250.00. The mortgage company was Fidelity Mortgage Company, and the interest rate on the loan was 5 percent, fixed rate.

On May 2, 2006, Eddi took out a loan on the property using Fast Cash Mortgage Company. The loan was for $75,000.00, and the interest rate was 4.8 percent but it was an adjustable rate mortgage, set to adjust every six months after the loan closed. The maximum interest adjustment was up to 15 percent. The proceeds of the loan were disbursed as follows:

a. $15,000.00 went to pay off the current mortgage with Fidelity. Fidelity Mortgage was two months behind at the time of the refinance with Fast Cash.
b. $1,000.00 went to pay the 2006 property taxes that were due.
c. $59,000.00 went to Eddi in cash. Eddi's plan was to invest the money in a new home that she could own by herself. Eddi paid off Cee's $1,500.00 credit card bill and bought her a $500.00 stove. Eddi kept the rest of the money.
d. Eddi was the only person who signed the promissory note, agreeing to pay back the money.
e. Cee signed the Deed of Trust, simply acknowledging that her home was being encumbered by the loan.

After the closing, Eddi bought a home in Cary, North Carolina. She used the remaining $57,000.00 as a down payment. In early 2007, Cee became sick and Eddi sold her home in Cary, North Carolina, and moved in with Cee to take care of her. The sale of the home produced no profit because the value of the home had deteriorated substantially since it was purchased.

Dee has also discovered that the interest rate on the current mortgage is set to adjust to 8.5 percent next month. The principal and interest payments will then be $1,650.00 per month. Dee cannot afford to pay half of the mortgage. Furthermore, Dee thinks it is unfair that she should have to pay one-half of the $74,000.00 mortgage balance when her mother only had a $15,000.00 mortgage. Dee wants to sue Fast Cash Mortgage only. She could never bring herself to sue Eddi, her mother's special friend.

Eddi stopped making the mortgage payments three months ago because she is frustrated about the entire situation. A foreclosure petition has been filed and is currently pending for the property in Monroe, North Carolina.

We want to advise Dee as to whether she can file an action against Fast Cash for violations of the N.C. Anti-Predatory Lending Act, based on her allegation that there was "loan flipping." We also want to know whether Dee can be the plaintiff in any potential action because, although she is now a co-owner of the property, Dee did not take out the loan. We have conducted preliminary research and determined that the only relevant cases are *Homeowner v. Ohno Federal Mortgage* and *Wally v. Homeaway Mortgage*. You have also found two statutes that seem to be helpful, N.C. Gen. Stat. §§ 24-2, 24-10.2(c). Prepare a memorandum based upon these two cases and statutes as they relate to the issues noted above.

IN THE UNITED STATES BANKRUPTCY COURT
FOR THE EASTERN DISTRICT OF NORTH CAROLINA
WILSON DIVISION

IN RE:
JUDY G. HOMEOWNER
Debtor.
Case No. 05-012345-8-JRL

JUDY G. HOMEOWNER
Plaintiff, vs.
Adversary Proceeding No.: 05-101-8-AP
OHNO FEDERAL MORTGAGE,
Defendant.

ORDER

This matter is before the court on the motion to dismiss filed by Defendant Ohno Mortgage ("Ohno Federal"). On February 2, 2006, the court conducted a hearing in Wilson, North Carolina.

FACTUAL BACKGROUND

On October 1, 2004, the Plaintiff contacted Ohno Federal Mortgage ("Ohno") to inquire about refinancing an existing mortgage on her residence. A representative from Ohno visited the Plaintiff and she filled out a loan application. On November 26, 2002, the Plaintiff executed a promissory note in favor of Ohno Federal secured by the Plaintiff's primary residence located in Edward, North Carolina (the "mortgage loan"). According to the HUD-1 Settlement Statement, the Plaintiff was charged fees in connection with her loan totaling $3,796.06. Plaintiff made timely payments on her original loan. In fact, Plaintiff never missed a payment, nor was she ever late on a payment. Plaintiff always paid her property taxes on time. However, Plaintiff sought the new loan because she was hoping to get a lower interest rate and she wanted money for home improvements.

PROCEDURAL HISTORY

On June 27, 2005, the Plaintiff filed a Chapter 13 bankruptcy petition in an effort to stop the sale of her home at a foreclosure. Ohno Federal filed a proof of claim in the case in the amount of $52,370.19. On August 30, 2005, the Plaintiff filed a complaint objecting to the secured claim asserted by Ohno Federal. The main cause of action asserted is an alleged violation of the North Carolina Anti-Predatory Lending Act, N.C.G.S. § 24-1.1A. The Plaintiff contends that Ohno Federal is subject to this claim because the mortgage loan is a "high-cost loan" under § 24-1.1E.

On November 30, 2005, Ohno Federal filed this motion to dismiss pursuant to Rule 12(b)(6) of the Federal Rules of Civil Procedure. In its brief in support of the motion, the Defendant asserts that the claims as alleged by Plaintiff are not legally cognizable. As such, the Defendant argues that the Plaintiff's claims under § 24-1 and N.C.G.S. § 75-1 should be dismissed.

DISCUSSION

I. Truth in Lending Act

The Truth in Lending Act ("TILA") is a federal statute that governs the terms and conditions of consumer loans, requiring lenders to make disclosures about loan fees and costs. See 15 U.S.C. § 1601 (2005). TILA was enacted to protect consumers from abusive practices in lending. See In re Cmty. Bank of N. Va. and Guar. Nat'l Bank of Tallahassee Second Mortgage Loan Litig., 418 F.3d 277, 303-04 (3d Cir. 2005). If a loan falls into the category of a high-cost loan, then the lender must provide the borrower with additional disclosures and home ownership counseling.

Plaintiff contends that Ohno failed to provide the appropriate home ownership counseling and Defendant asserts that such counseling was not required. Such home ownership counseling would have been provided by a certified housing counselor. Plaintiff would have had the opportunity to review the terms of the loan with a neutral party to ensure she understood what she was signing.

The Court acknowledges that Defendant's Motion to Dismiss is not based on TILA. However, when determining if the state laws have been violated, the Court will assess whether the safeguards of TILA should have been followed.

II. State Law Claims

The Plaintiff is asserting claims against the Defendant based on the North Carolina Anti-Predatory Lending Act.

Under Chapter 24 of the North Carolina General Statutes, every borrower must receive an actual benefit from the refinance of a loan. N.C. Gen. Stat. § 24-1 et seq. (2007). In other words, the new loan must be better than the old loan. The legislature has used the term "net, tangible benefit" but the term has not been defined further.

Plaintiff argues that the loan falls under the terms of the anti-predatory laws because the Plaintiff alleges that the loan provided no net, tangible benefit to her. Plaintiff contends that she is in a worse financial position because of the new loan. If it is in fact true that

Plaintiff has not received a net, tangible benefit as a result of the refinance, Plaintiff will have a viable claim against Defendant.

A. Higher interest rate

Plaintiff alleges that her initial interest rate was 8.5 percent and it was a two-year adjustable rate. When Plaintiff refinanced with Ohno, her interest rate was 8.0 percent and it was a six-month adjustable rate. On the face of the loan documents 8.5 percent is higher than 8.0 percent. However, at the time the loan went into foreclosure two years after the loan closed, the interest rate being charged by Ohno had adjusted three times, bringing the interest rate to 10.0 percent. If Plaintiff had maintained her original mortgage, the interest rate would only have adjusted once, bringing the interest rate to 9.0 percent. All parties will acknowledge that Ohno's interest rate adjusts at a faster rate that Plaintiff's original mortgage would have adjusted. We all must acknowledge that Plaintiff took a calculated risk when she agreed to accept an adjustable rate mortgage. The court must consider whether this was a knowing and fully disclosed risk. Further, in the absence of the home ownership counseling, is it an unfair trade practice for the borrower to appreciate the fact that an 8.0 percent interest rate may ultimately be higher than an 8.5 percent interest rate?

In deciding on the viability of this claim, the Court is persuaded by the fact that Plaintiff is an unsophisticated, uneducated borrower. Loan transactions are generally complicated, but when we delve into issues such as the rate of adjustability of an adjustable rate mortgage, the issues may not be clear to a borrower who lacks knowledge of real estate transactions.

B. Other benefits

Furthermore, Ohno argues that Plaintiff cannot assert that she derived no net, tangible benefit from the loan because she obtained $30,000.00 as a cash distribution at the loan closing. When Plaintiff refinanced, the $30,000.00 was given to her from the loan proceeds. These funds were used for adding a room on to the property. Plaintiff acknowledges that she received the cash-out. She also acknowledges that the new room was added to her property. She has benefited from the room addition.

Plaintiff has presented evidence that when the first loan is compared to Ohno's loan with the more rapidly adjusting interest rate, Plaintiff will ultimately pay $62,000.00 in additional interest over the life of the Ohno loan. In other words, had Plaintiff kept the original loan, she would have paid the home off for $62,000.00 less than she will pay off the Ohno loan. Plaintiff argues that while she received $30,000.00, it is not a benefit when the $30,000.00 cost her $62,000.00.

It is a unique situation when someone gets a fairly large amount of cash, but subsequently argues that she has received no benefit. However, it is also not clear whether $62,000.00 is a fair payment for $30,000.00.

Accordingly, the Court will decline to dismiss the causes of action.

CONCLUSION

Consequently, the Defendant's motion to dismiss Plaintiff's adversarial proceeding is denied.

UNITED STATES BANKRUPTCY COURT
EASTERN DISTRICT OF NORTH CAROLINA
RALEIGH DIVISION

IN RE:
ALICE U. WALLY DEBTOR
CASE NO. 07-1906-5-ATS

ALICE U. WALLY
Plaintiff v.
HOMEAWAY FINANCIAL NETWORK, INC.
Defendant.

ADVERSARY PROCEEDING NO.
S-07-1908-5-AP

ORDER DENYING MOTION TO DISMISS AND
DENYING MOTION FOR RELIEF FROM STAY

The matters before the court are the motion to dismiss this adversary proceeding filed by the Defendant's Homeaway Financial Network, Inc., and the Bank of New York Trust Company, N.A., and the motion for relief from the automatic stay filed by Homeaway. A hearing took place in Raleigh, North Carolina, on June 12, 2007.

Alice U. Wally filed a petition for relief under Chapter 13 of the Bankruptcy Code on February 22, 2007. Ms. Wally is a co-owner with her daughter, Theresa Wally, of property at 306 New Rolly Road, Garner, North Carolina. Prior to October 2002, the debtor and her daughter were obligated on a debt secured by the residence. On October 3, 2002, Theresa Wally refinanced the debt through Coaxing Acceptance Corporation. Homeaway now owns the refinanced loan and seeks relief from the automatic stay to pursue a foreclosure action it initiated in 2005, contending that no payments have been received since April 2005, and that the loan is due from December 2004. Ms. Wally filed the instant adversary proceeding alleging that the Defendants violated North Carolina General Statutes §§ 24-10.2(c) and 24-8(d), having "flipped" a consumer home loan, and charged fees and interest greater than those allowed by law. Ms. Wally also contends that these acts were unfair and deceptive trade practices actionable under Chapter 75 of the North Carolina General Statutes.

The Defendants seek dismissal of the adversary proceeding pursuant to Rule 12(b)(6) of the Federal Rules of Civil Procedure, made applicable to this proceeding by Rule 7012(b) of the Federal Rules of Bankruptcy Procedure. The Defendants maintain that §§ 24-10.2 and 24-8 apply only to a "borrower" who incurred the debt in question, and that because Ms. Wally is not an obligor on the loan, she has no remedy under these statutes. Ms. Wally contends that because the loan encumbers her property she is in effect a "borrower" and may seek relief under those statutes. Both parties acknowledge that the statute does not define "borrower" or "debt."

Section 24-2, which establishes the penalty for usury and allows usury to be raised as a counterclaim to a foreclosure action, specifically provides that:

> If security has been given for an usurious loan and the debtor *or other person having an interest in the security* seeks relief against the enforcement of the security or seeks any other affirmative relief, the debtor or other person having an interest in the security shall not be required to pay or to offer to pay the principal plus legal interest as a condition to obtaining the relief sought but shall be entitled to the advantages provided in this section.

N.C. Gen. Stat. § 24-2 (emphasis added).

Clearly, Ms. Wally has standing to pursue relief under that section and any other provision to which that section relates. Section 24-10.2(e) provides that § 24-10.2 (the consumer protection for home loans statute) may be enforced by "any party to a consumer home loan," which may be broad enough to encompass a signatory to the deed of trust who is not an obligor on the note. The consumer protection statutes at issue should be construed broadly, and in the absence of limiting language in the statute, the court finds that it does extend to Ms. Wally. Accordingly, the motion to dismiss will be denied. Ms. Wally is a co-owner of the property in question. Ms. Wally signed certain documents, including the Deed of Trust and Notice of Right to Rescission. Ms. Wally never signed the Promissory Note, which would have obligated her to repay the loan. Ms. Wally has lived at the home in question for over 40 years. Surely, she has an interest in the preservation of the property.

The court will revisit this issue in approximately 60 days to determine whether further relief may be appropriate.

Based on the foregoing, the Defendants' motion to dismiss and Homeaway's motion for relief from the automatic stay are **DENIED**. The motion for relief from the automatic stay will be reviewed in approximately 60 days.

SO ORDERED.

ISSUE IDENTIFICATION

After reading the memo, we are clear on the client's objectives. Dee wants to sue the mortgage company. The memo problem states:

We want to advise Dee as to whether she can file an action against Fast Cash for violations of the N.C. Anti-Predatory Lending Act, based on her allegation that there was "loan flipping." We also want to know whether Dee can be the Plaintiff in any potential action because, although she is now a co-owner of the property, Dee did not take out the loan.

The two issues to research have practically been stated for us. Yet still, even if the issues were not strongly suggested in the memo problem, after reading the *Homeowner* case, we must begin to question what makes a loan beneficial. It appears obvious that if an interest rate is lowered, then the homeowner received a benefit. However, *Homeowner* makes us question what is really a benefit. Similarly, we see facts in the memo problem that make us question whether Dee's mother, Cee, received a benefit.

After reading *Wally*, we begin to wonder if Dee is really a party who can sue the lender. Dee did not own the property at the time Cee and Eddi obtained the loan. It appears that the contract is between the lenders and the homeowners, Cee and Eddi. However, *Wally* makes us wonder who can bring a cause of action and under what circumstances.

Issue Statement One
What is the law you will reference?
What is the legal question you need to answer?
What are the facts that have brought the legal question into dispute?

Under the North Carolina Anti-Predatory Lending law [N.C. Gen. Stat. § 24-1 *et seq.*], is Dee considered the borrower (plaintiff, debtor, or other person of interest having standing to sue) when she is the sole heir to her mother's estate and her mother owned a one-half interest in her home and her mother's home was encumbered by a mortgage, but her mother never signed the promissory note?

Or

The issue is whether, under the North Carolina Anti-Predatory Lending law [N.C. Gen. Stat. § 24-1 *et seq.*], Dee is considered the borrower (plaintiff, debtor, or other person of interest having standing to sue) when she is the sole heir to her mother's estate and her mother owned a one-half interest in her home and her mother's home was encumbered by a mortgage, but her mother never signed the promissory note.

Issue Statement Two
What is the law you will reference?
What is the legal question you need to answer?
What are the facts that have brought the legal question into dispute?

Under the North Carolina Anti-Predatory Lending law [N.C. Gen. Stat. § 24-1 *et seq.*], did Cee (or Cee and Eddi or Dee or the co-owner) receive a net, tangible (or tangible, net) benefit from the loan transaction when: 1) Cee had a $15,000.00 mortgage on the property that was two months behind; 2) the loan paid Cee's 2006 property taxes; 3) Cee's $1,500.00 credit card was paid; 4) Cee received a stove; 5) the original loan had a fixed interest rate; 6) the new loan had an adjustable rate and 7) the actual borrower received $59,000.00?

Or

The issue is whether, under the North Carolina Anti-Predatory Lending law [N.C. Gen. Stat. § 24-1 *et seq.*], Cee (or Cee and Eddi or Dee or the co-owner) receive a net, tangible (or tangible, net) when: 1) Cee had a $15,000.00 mortgage on the property that was two months behind; 2) the loan paid Cee's 2006 property taxes; 3) Cee's $1,500.00 credit card was paid; 4) Cee received a stove; 5) the original loan had a fixed interest rate; 6) the new loan had an adjustable rate and 7) the actual borrower received $59,000.00.

STATEMENT OF FACTS

Each memorandum requires a summary of the facts. In an objective memorandum, the facts should be stated objectively, succinctly, and accurately. Include all of the legally significant facts.

Key: If there is a fact that you will discuss in your analysis, you need to discuss it in the "Facts" section of your memorandum.

List the facts you think were significant and then compare them to the facts that are listed on the next page.

Dee is the sole beneficiary of Cee's estate.
Cee and Eddi owned the property as joint tenants in common.
Cee had a $15,000.00 mortgage on the property.
Eddi took out a $75,000.00 mortgage on the property.
Cee's interest rate on the $15,000.00 mortgage was 5.0 percent, fixed.
Eddi's interest rate on the $75,000.00 mortgage was 4.8 percent, adjustable.
Eddi took $57,000.00 of the loan proceeds and used it to buy a home.
The new loan's interest rate is set to adjust to 8.5 percent.
Cee's $15,000.00 loan was paid off when Eddi took out the new loan.
Cee's loan payment was $250.00 and the new loan payment is $1,500.00 and will increase to $1,650.00.

ANALYSIS

This is the bread-and-butter of the memorandum. The CRAC is preferred. You are encouraged to conclude early and often. After the conclusion, you need to state a synthesized rule, otherwise known as the general principle.

Key: An ideal synthesized rule includes the case law and the statute.

This is a general rule and not literally every rule you wish to discuss in the case discussions. The rule is a statement and/or application of the statutory provision(s) and case law, i.e., What do §24-2 and §24-10.2 provide, and what further information is found in the cases? Give a general statement of rules as a forecast of the analysis. There should be a separate statement at the beginning of the discussion of each issue.

What do you think the general rule is here?

Discussion of the Cases

After you have stated your conclusion and your synthesized rule, you can get into the case discussions for the issue you are addressing. Always start with the case facts, then case holding, and the rationale for the holding. Never discuss comparisons and contrasts between the precedent case and the current case before you have addressed the facts, holding, and rationale for the holding of the precedent cases.

What are the key facts in *Wally*?

In Re Alice U. Wally

Key facts: Ms. Wally owned her home as a joint tenant with her daughter. Ms. Wally had lived in the home for many years. Ms. Wally's daughter, Theresa, took out a new loan on the home. Ms. Wally never signed a document acknowledging that she would pay for the new loan, the promissory note. Ms. Wally did sign some documents to acknowledge the existence of the loan, the deed of trust.

What was the court's holding and why?

Holding and rationale: Ms. Wally could be considered a "borrower" (debtor or other person with interest) under the statute, even though she never signed a promissory note, because she has an ownership interest in the property. The term "borrower" should be construed broadly.

What are the relevant facts in *Homeowner*?

In Re Judy G. Homeowner

Key facts: Homeowner refinanced her mortgage to get a lower interest rate and to get money to make home improvements. Homeowner obtained a mortgage with an 8.0 percent interest rate that adjusts every six months. Homeowner's previous mortgage interest rate was 8.5 percent, but it adjusted every two years. The current mortgage interest rate had adjusted to 9.0 percent. Homeowner received $30,000.00 in cash when she refinanced her home.

What was the court's holding and why?

Holding: Homeowner presented a viable argument regarding whether she received a net, tangible benefit from the refinance. While Homeowner received $30,000.00 in cash to make home improvements, the interest rate on the new loan adjusted faster than her previous loan and will ultimately cost her more money.

Analogies

Once you have explained the case facts, holding, and rationale for the holding, then you can compare and contrast the precedent case from the present case presented in the memo problem. Remember that you need only to address the analogies and distinctions that impact the analysis.

What are the relevant analogies in the cases?

In Re Alice U. Wally

1. In both cases, the home was owned by two people as joint tenants.
2. In both cases, only one of the co-owners took out the refinanced loan.
Alice and Dee/Cee had significant connections to the property. Alice and Cee signed the deeds of trust, not the promissory notes.

In Re Judy G. Homeowner

1. In both cases, the person who took out the loan received a large cash payment.
2. In both cases, the new loan had an adjustable interest rate.
Other relevant analogies: e.g., in both cases, the new loan started out at a lower interest rate than the previous loan, but then increased to a higher interest rate than the previous loan.

Distinctions

What are the relevant distinctions in the cases?

In Re Alice U. Wally

In *Wally*, Ms. Wally owned the home at the time of the refinance. In the present case, Dee did not own the home at the time of the refinance, but inherited her interest later.

Dee did not sign the deed of trust. Alice signed the deed of trust. 2) Dee did not own an interest in the property at the time of the refinance. Alice owned an interest in the property at the time of the refinance. Etc.

In Re Judy G. Homeowner

In *Homeowner*, the borrower had an adjustable rate on the original loan.

In the present case, Cee had a fixed interest rate.

Other relevant distinctions: e.g., differences in the use of the money, differences in education level, etc.

CONCLUSION

At the end of the document, you are to conclude again. This conclusion should sound very similar to the mini-conclusions you had at the beginning and end of each of your issues, assuming you used the CRAC method. Additionally, if there is a strong public policy supporting your position, the conclusion would be the appropriate place to insert that brief policy discussion.

What would be the policies that are addressed in this memo problem?

The government has an interest in protecting homeowners from predatory lending practices.